THE NARROW GAUGE RAILWAYS OF FINISTERE

PETER SMITH

ISBN-13: 978-1532917752

ISBN-10: 1532917759

COPYRIGHT PETER SMITH 2016

This book is dedicated to my friend John Dale who gave me a book on the railways of Finistere after he'd been on holiday there, which sparked my interest in the area.

I was frustrated that nothing was available in English, so the obvious answer was to do the research and write it myself!

All the pictures in this book are from the author's collection, are used with permission or were taken by the author.

CONTENTS

1. **INTROUDUCTION   PAGE 4**
2. **THE STANDARD GAUGE ROUTES   PAGE 5**
3. **THE RESEAU BRETON   PAGE 11**
4. **THE FIRST NETWORK.   PAGE 13**
5. **THE SECOND NETWORK.   PAGE 16**
6. **LOCO'S AND ROLLING STOCK.   PAGE 19**
7. **NORTHERN FINISTERE   PAGE 29**

BREST TO PORTSALL   PAGE 30

BREST TO L'ABER-WRAC'H   PAGE 43

PLABENNEC TO LESNEVEN   PAGE 51

LANDERNEAU RO BRIGNOGAN   PAGE 58

PLOUIDER TO PLOUESCAT AND ST POL.   PAGE 60

CHATEAUNEUF DU FAOU TO LANDIVISIAU AND PLOUESCAT   PAGE 64

MORLAIX TO PRIMEL.   PAGE 69

8. **SOUTHERN FINISTERE   PAGE 81**

DOUARNENEZ TO AUDIERNE   PAGE 82

PONT L'ABBE TO ST GUENOLE   PAGE 89

CONCARNEAU TO QUIMPERLE   PAGE 94

PONT CROIX TO PONT L'ABBE   PAGE 101

ROSPORDEN TO CHATEAUNEUF DU FOU   PAGE 102

9. **BIBLIOGRAPHY   PAGE 105**

INTRODUCTION

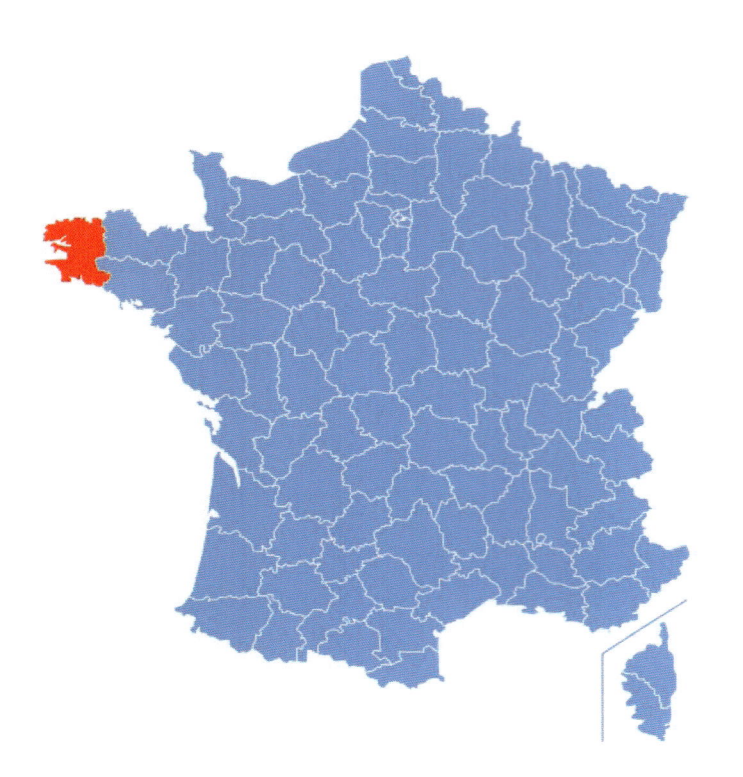

The coat of Arms of Finistere; the flag is similar.

The name Finistere means literally 'the end of the earth', derived from the Latin 'terrae' in a similar way as Lands End in Cornwall. The Breton translation however can also mean 'head of the world' so it rather depends on your point of view! There is no connection with Finnisterre in Spain, other than the similarity in the names.

Finistere is one of the four departments that make up modern Brittany and is where the Breton language is still most commonly spoken with many Breton schools teaching it alongside French. Finistere is the most westerly part of mainland France and has a long, rugged and exposed coastline.

Not surprisingly it took a while for main line railways to penetrate Finistere but the port of Brest was an obvious destination and both the Ouest and Paris Orleans railways built lines into the department, the Ouest from Rennes reaching Brest in 1865.

The metre gauge Reseau Breton system was centred on Carhaix which is just inside the department and lines radiated out from there, reaching Camaret, Morlaix and Rosporden. That still left a lot of Finistere without any railways though, and it is the narrow gauge lines that were built from 1893 onwards to serve these towns and villages that are the subject of this book. The Reseau Breton is well know and has been the subject of numerous books and articles but the other lines have passed into history virtually unnoticed, leaving few tangible remains. The book collects as much information about them as possible and presents it for the first time in English.

THE STANDARD GAUGE ROUTES IN FINISTERE.

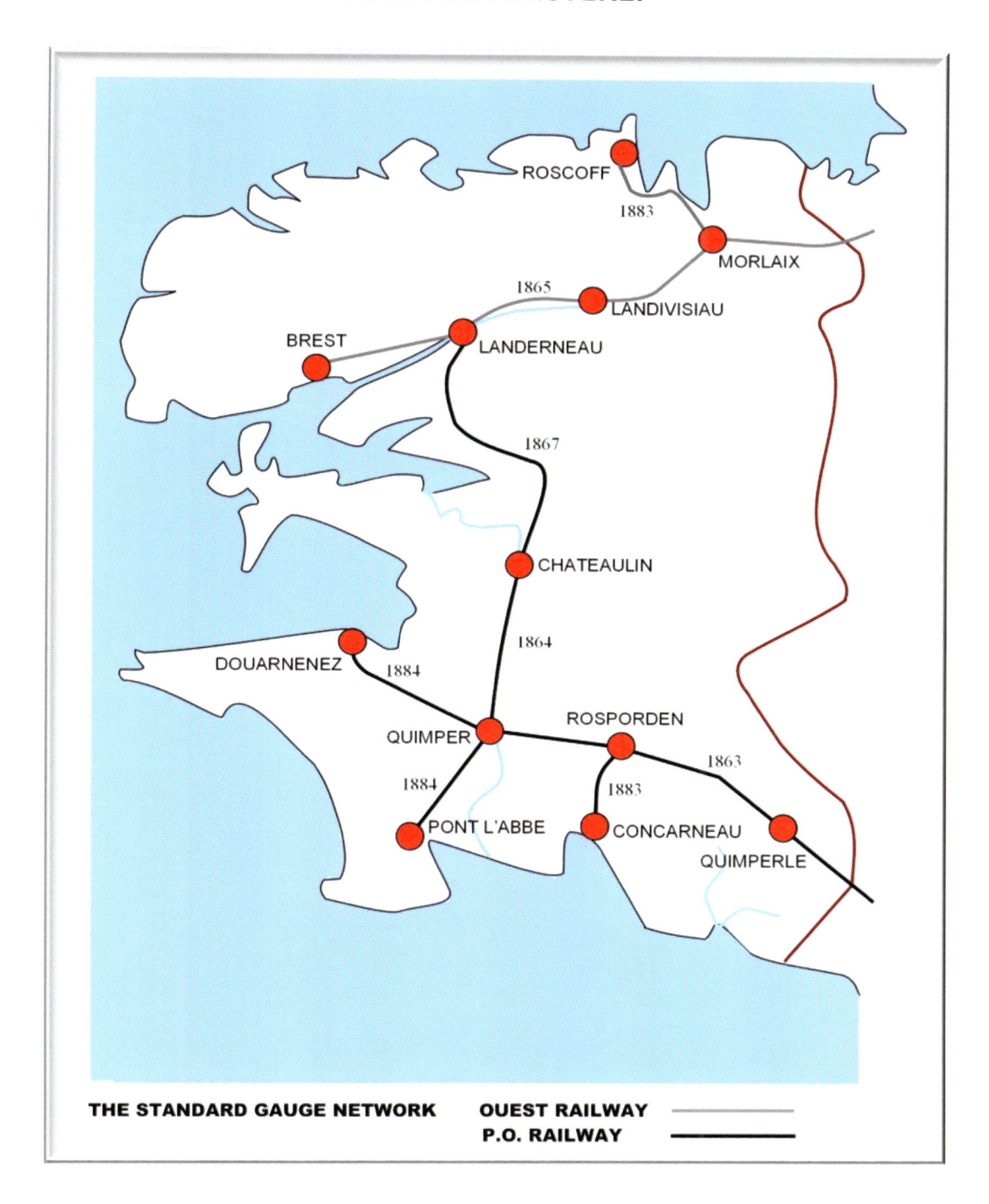

The Paris Orleans Railway and the Ouest Railway both reached Finistere in the mid 1860's, the final sections of main line originating in Paris. Both routes aimed for the coast and the port towns, especially Brest and Roscoff which were both served by the Ouest. The companies did not indulge in unnecessary duplication, the PO remaining in the south other than for building a line to Landerneau on the Ouest main line.

Morlaix station, which was shared between the Ouest which built it in 1865 and the Reseau Breton.

The Ouest Railway main line to Brest wasn't a cheap one to build as it crossed the valleys rather than making use of them, resulting in structures such as the superb viaduct at Morlaix.

The magnificent station at Brest from the approach road.

183. BREST — La Grande Gare

The Ouest station of 1865 was demolished and replaced with this very modern building in 1932 by the Etat Railway.

The standard gauge lines have not been immune to closure; this is St Pol de Leon on the Ouest branch to Roscoff. There was once a connection to the CFDF narrow gauge here, but now the line is just clinging onto life with only three return trips per day in summer and two in winter. A viaduct is unsafe and there is no money to repair it, resulting in scenes such as the bottom picture. Technically the station is open, but you wouldn't think so.

A support group has been formed to promote the line, so maybe the future is looking a little brighter.

Quimper station on the Paris Orleans Railway line that runs across the south of Finistere.

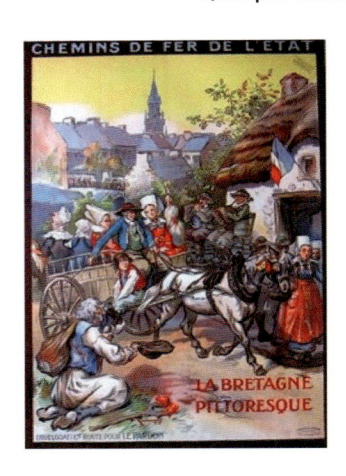

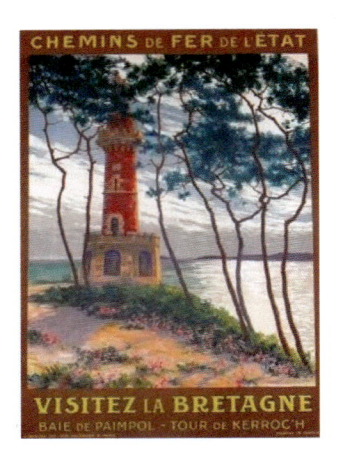

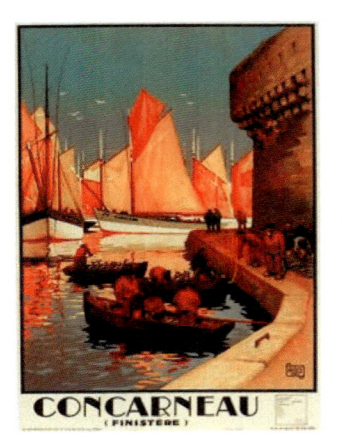

The main line railways went to great lengths to promote Finistere.

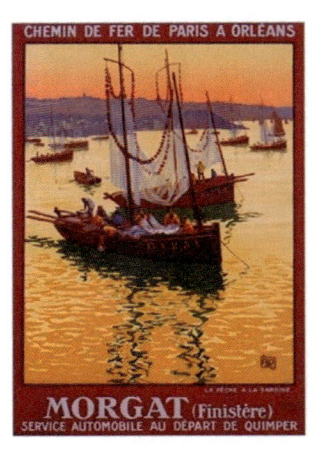

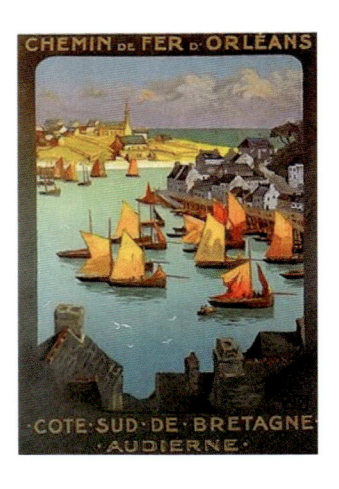

THE RESEAU BRETON

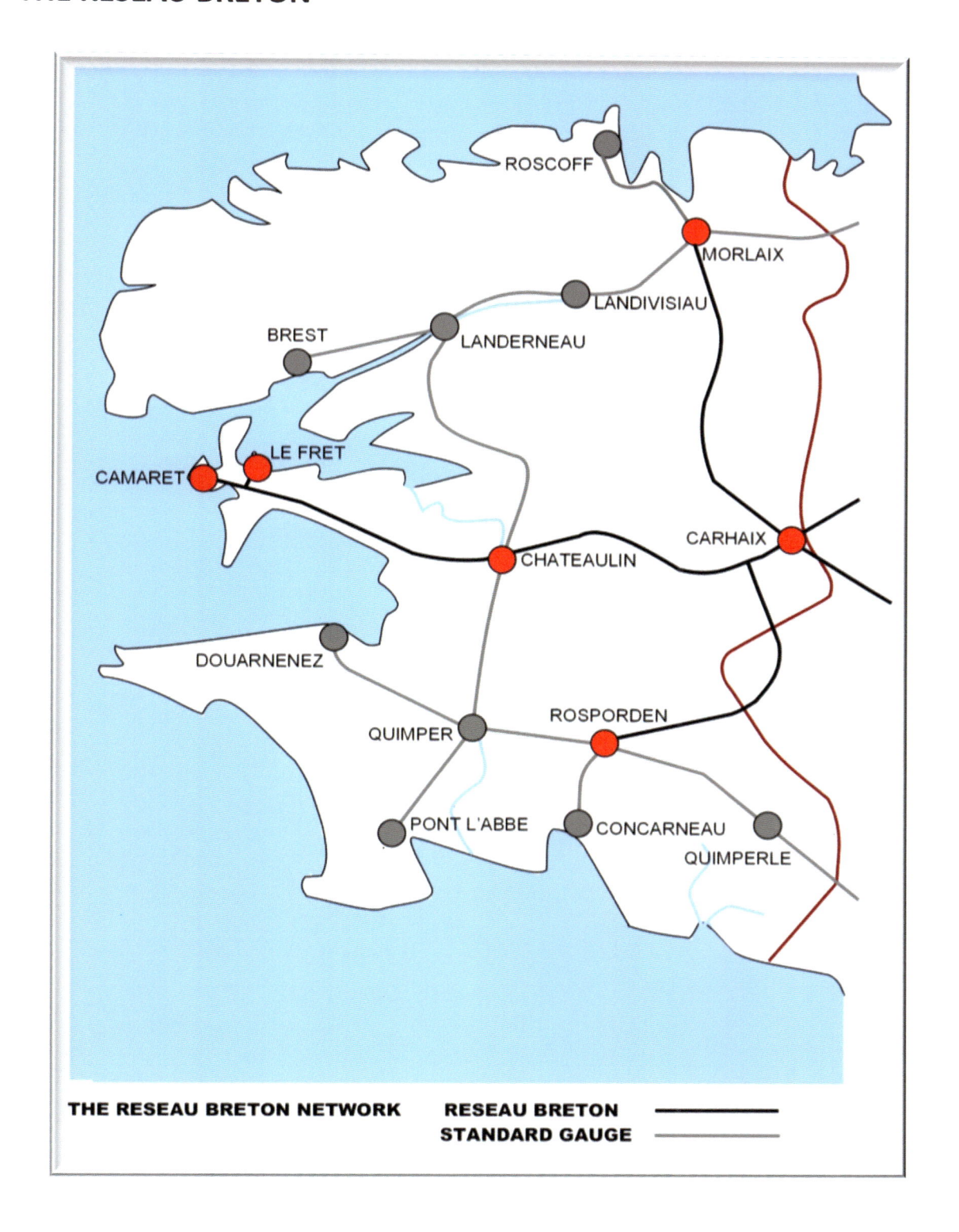

The concession to build a system of metre gauge local railways serving Brittany was granted in 1880 to the Ouest railway, with the provision that should the need arise the lines could be converted to standard gauge. The offices would be in Morlaix, but the engineering centre would be at the hub of the system in Carhaix.

When the railway was constructed it was as a separate company, the Reseau Breton, though links with the Ouest were always close to the extent of sharing stations and facilities. The first route opened in 1891 and by the time the last line had opened in 1925 there was 428km of track. Closure to passengers began in 1939 but the system lasted far longer than most French narrow gauge railways; the last metre gauge lines closed in 1967, but Morlaix to Carhaix and Paimpol were both converted to standard gauge and remain open today.

This book will not go into detail about the Reseau Breton as it has been widely covered already in English and French; for details see the Bibliography. However, it cannot be ignored as it connected in several places with the CFDF and the CFA lines and those places will be described fully in later chapters.

Carhaix station, the hub of the Reseau Breton system.

Typical Reseau Breton station architecture at Mael station. Note how it has been laid out to allow relaying as standard gauge if that was required.

One of the superb Mallet loco's is preserved at Carhaix.

12

THE FIRST NETWORK 1893 TO 1909

CHEMINS DE FER DU FINISTERE.

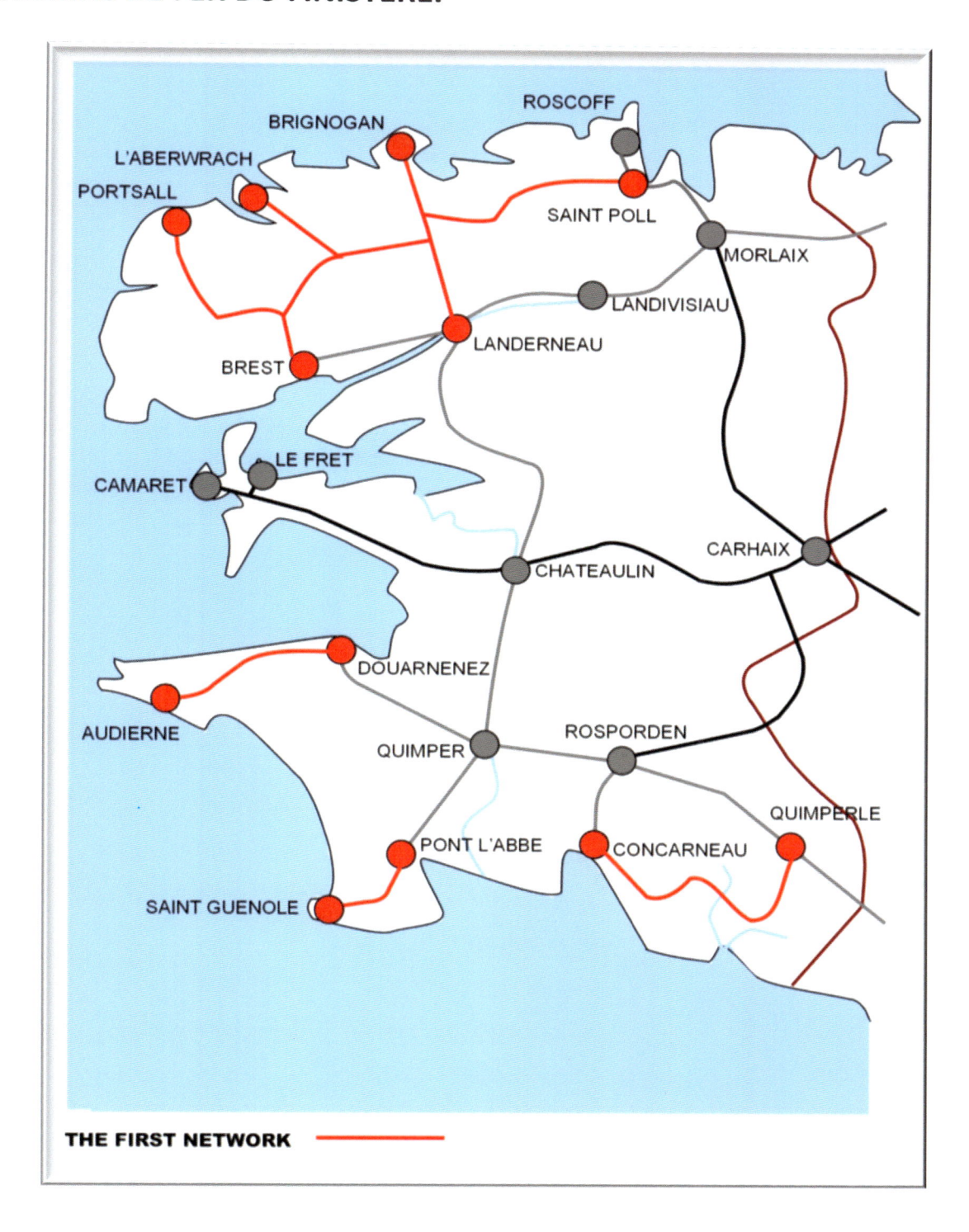

CHEMINS DE FER DEPARTMENTAUX DU FINISTERE

The idea of creating a network of local railways serving Finistere was first mooted in 1888, and the importance of improving connections to the fishing ports along the coast was uppermost in the minds of those involved in the discussions. After much consideration the Declaration of Public Utility was declared in 1891 and the creation of the network passed from being simply an idea to an concrete proposal that was being acted upon.

Six firms tendered for the work, five of them contractors, but the job was given to the sixth, the *Société d'Études et Concessions de Chemins de fer d'intérêt local et de Tramways*. There was some nepotism involved as the president of the company was Armand Rousseau, and his nephew and Godson was the first president of the CdF Departmentaux du Finistere! That wasn't just a coincidence.

The first six lines were given their DUP on 14th February 1891 but it was soon realised that a more comprehensive network would be needed, especially as the first lines did not reach the sea which was the whole idea in the first place. Further routes were added to the plan though they did not receive their DUP until 1898 and later, extending the system to Aberwrac'h and Brignogan.

The first two lines opened in 1893 and the next four in 1894, after which came a period of consolidation as the next lines would not open for another five years. The company had to get used to running the service and all that entailed so six routes were plenty to begin with. In 1896, though, Armand Rousseau died and the caution that had prevailed died with him; what can only be described as euphoria swept through the company and they began planning routes here there and everywhere with very little regard for the potential of making any profit. This feeling prevailed until 1914, although the Department did bring some much needed realism as their budget wasn't unlimited.

The lines that were completed up to 1909 comprise the first network:

BREST TO SAINT RENAN	OPENED May 24th 1893	CLOSED	1935.	17km
SAINT RENAN TO PLOUDAIMEZEAU	July 14th 1893		1935	14km
DOUARNENEZ TO AUDIERNE	January 29th 1894		1946	20km
LA RUFA TO PLPLABENNEC	February 26th 1894		1946	24km
PLABENNEC TO LANNILIS	February 26th 1894		1932	24km
LANDERNEAU TO PLOUNEOUR	June 11th 1894		1946	27km
PLOUDALMEZEAU TO PORTSALL	July 14th 1899		1935	4km
LANNILIS TO L'ABER-WRAC'H	February 25th 1900		1932	6km
PLOUENOUR TO BRIGNOGAN	August 11th 1901		1946	2km
QUIMPERLE TO PONT AVEN	March 9th 1903		1936	21km
PLABENNEC TO LESNEVEN	February 14th 1904		1946	13km
PLOUIDER TO PLOUESCAT	July 11th 1904		1946	15km
PLOUESCAT TO SAINT POL	July 1st 1907		1946	15km
PONT L'ABBE TO ST GUENOLE	July 4th 1907		1947	18km
PONT AVEN TO CONCARNEAU	June 14th 1908		1936	17km
CONCARNEAU VILLE TO P.O. STATION	December 1st 1909		1936	1km

HORAIRE DES TRAINS — Service d'Été

Pont-l'Abbé à Quimper

	mat.	mat.	soir	soir	soir
Pont-l'Abbé (d.)	5 55	11 25	1 4	3 19	7 21
Combrit-Tréméoc	7 3	11 39	1 17	3 32	7 31
Pluguffan	7 19	11 54	1 28	3 48	7 43
Quimper (arr.)	7 34	12 13	1 43	4 06	7 58

Quimper à Pont-l'Abbé

	mat.	mat.	mat.	soir	soir	soir
Quimper (dép)	5 25	8 21	10 30	12 45	6 4	8 53
Pluguffan	5 50	»	10 47	1 2	6 21	9 10
Combrit-Tréméoc	7 10	»	10 58	1 16	6 32	9 20
Pont-l'Abbé a.	7 23	8 56	11 07	1 25	6 41	9 30

Pont-l'Abbé à Saint-Guénolé-Penmarc'h

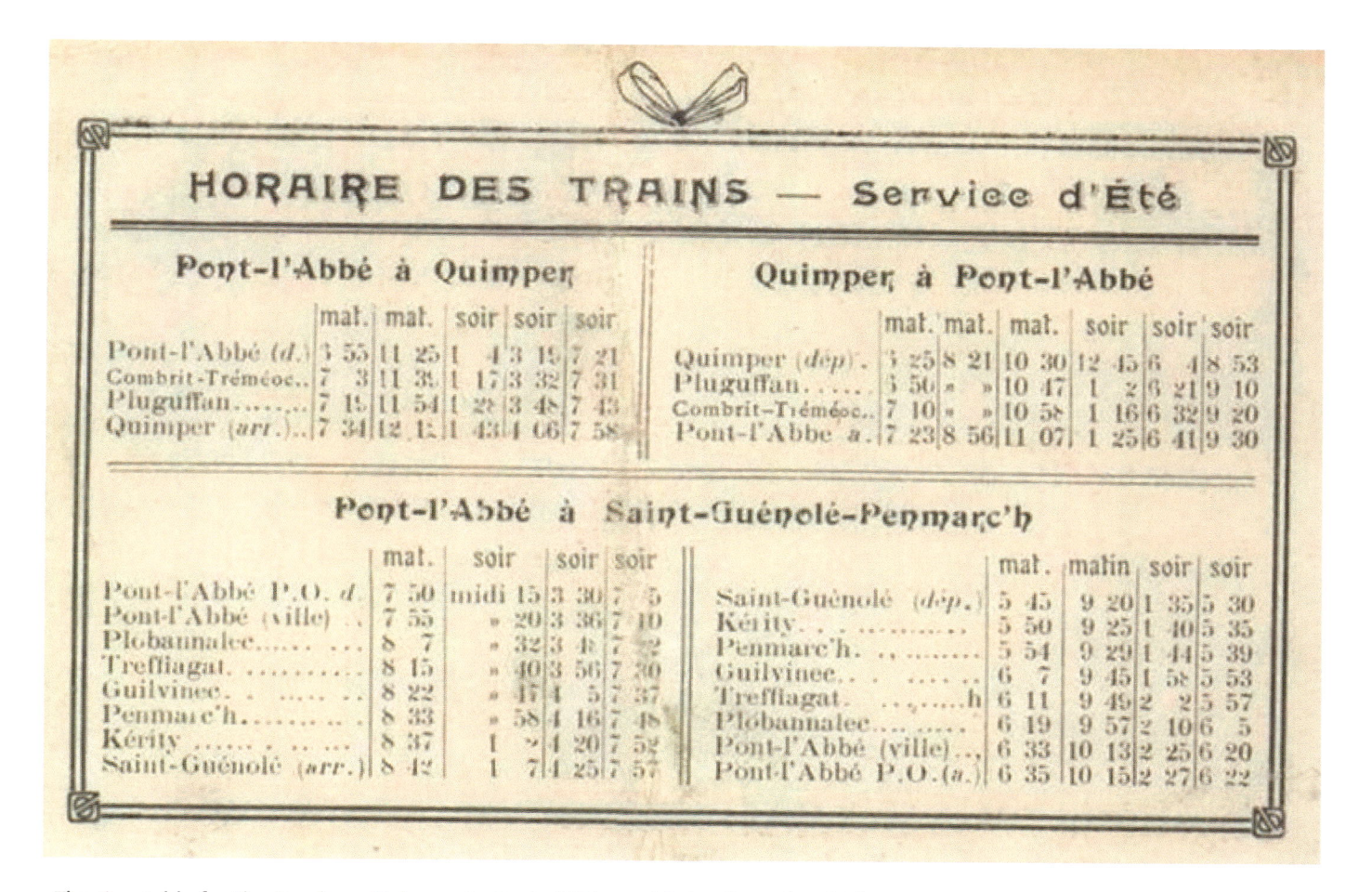

	mat.	soir	soir	soir
Pont-l'Abbé P.O. d.	7 50	midi 15	3 30	7 5
Pont-l'Abbé (ville)	7 55	» 20	3 36	7 10
Plobannalec	8 7	» 32	3 48	7 22
Treffiagat	8 15	» 40	3 56	7 30
Guilvinec	8 22	» 47	4 5	7 37
Penmarc'h	8 33	» 58	4 16	7 48
Kérity	8 37	1 2	4 20	7 52
Saint-Guénolé (arr.)	8 42	1 7	4 25	7 57

	mat.	matin	soir	soir
Saint-Guénolé (dép.)	5 45	9 20	1 35	5 30
Kérity	5 50	9 25	1 40	5 35
Penmarc'h	5 54	9 29	1 44	5 39
Guilvinec	6 7	9 45	1 58	5 53
Treffiagat	6 11	9 49	2 2	5 57
Plobannalec	6 19	9 57	2 10	6 5
Pont-l'Abbé (ville)	6 33	10 13	2 25	6 20
Pont-l'Abbé P.O. (a.)	6 35	10 15	2 27	6 22

The timetable for the line from Quimper to Pont L'Abbe and Saint Guenole which was pretty typical of those in place across the system. Between Quimper and Pont L'Abbe there was quite a decent service, but of course that was on the standard gauge branch of the P.O. railway.

One the CFDF line there was a departure at 07.50, connecting with the first arrival from Quimper, arriving in St Guenole at 08.42 with six stops along the way. That was fifty two minutes for a journey of 18km, including the stops, which goes some way to explain why the narrow gauge found it so difficult to compete with the bus by the 1930's.

There were four trains each way on the narrow gauge which was no doubt ample and they were well spaced out though you do wonder how much demand there was for a departure at quarter to six in the morning. The line would only have required one loco to run the service and trains would have been mixed so no additional freight trains would have been needed.

The loco ended up at St Guenole at 7.57pm, so it must have been shedded there overnight.

7128 PONT-L'ABBÉ - Le petit train pour Penmarch

THE SECOND NETWORK 1912 AND 1913

CHEMINS DE FER ARMORICAINS

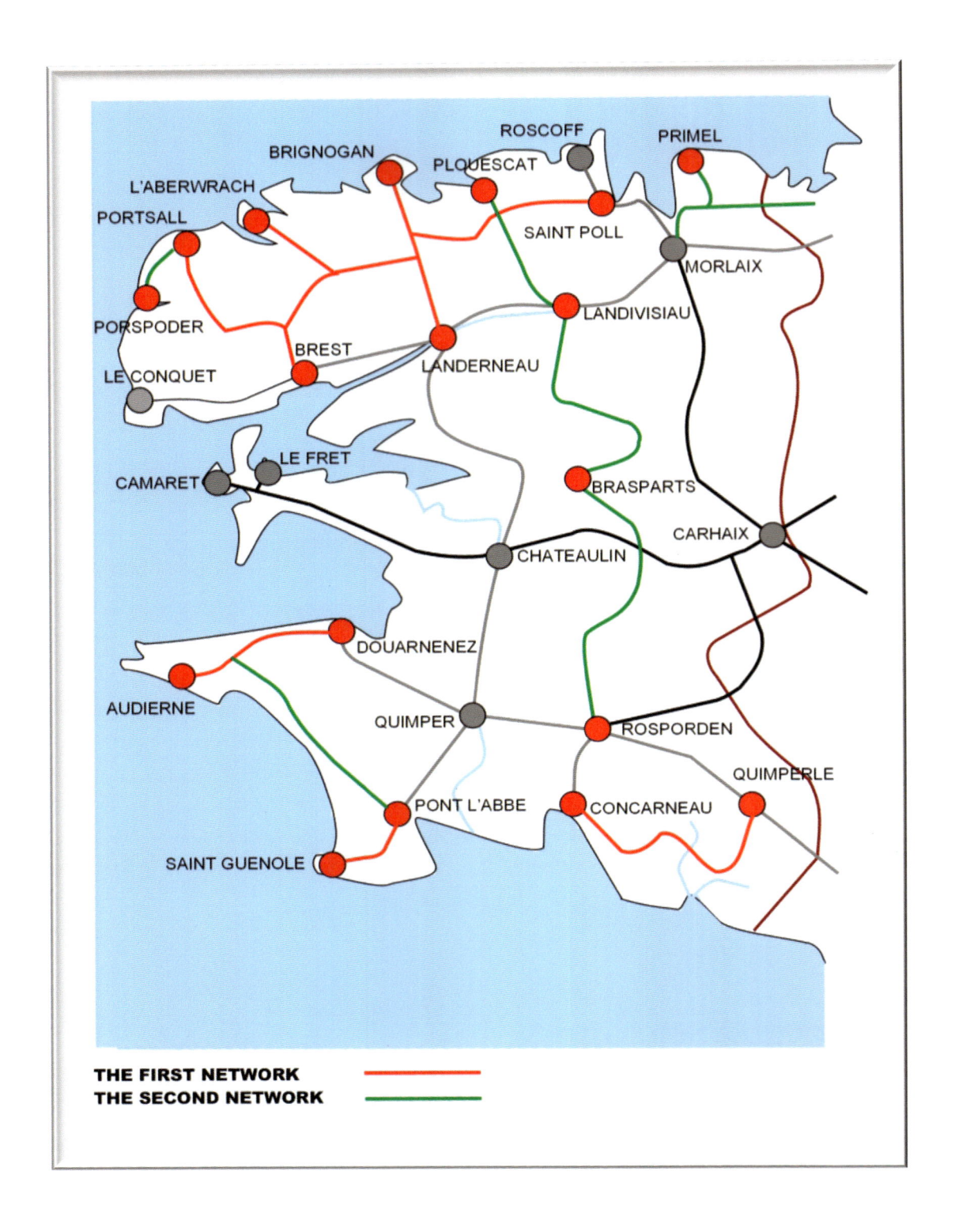

CHEMINS DE FER ARMORICAINS.

In 1905, although work was well under way on the lines that were already planned it became evident that once they were open there were no new schemes in the planning stages to take their place. In 1906 thoughts turned to whether it was plausible to construct any further lines and amazingly new proposals totalling 500km of routes were brought forward. These would in due course become the second network.

Not surprisingly the finance department were less than impressed with this sort of thinking, and a large dose of cold water was poured over the idea. The first four lines that had been proposed, though, did go forward for consideration and were passed. One shudders to think where the lines that were thrown out were planned to go!

In order to build the new lines a new limited company was formed by M. Favre who had tendered in competition with the CFDF. The Department felt that by creating a second company to build the new lines it would avoid having a powerful monopoly but in fact the two companies worked so closely together that they may as well have been a single entity. They couldn't have operated the system any other way, having to share stations and indeed whole sections of line.

Nevertheless, the Chemins de Fer Armoricains came into existence and built the second network as follows:

PORTSALL TO PORSPODER	OPENED May 13th 1913	CLOSED 1935	8km
MORLAIX TO PRIMEL	May 1st 1912	1934	22km
PLOUEZOCH TO PONT MENOU	March 1st 1913	1932	14km
PLOUESCAT TO LANDIVISIAU VILLE	November 10th 1912	1946	24km
LANDIVISIAU TO LA FEUILLEE	June 11th 1912	1933	34km
LA FEUILLEE TO CHATEAUNEUF	November 25th 1912	1933	38km
CHATEAUNEUF TO ROSPORDEN	December 21st 1912	1933	39km
PONT L'ABBE TO PONT CROIX	October 1st 1912	1933	35km

To think that almost all those lines opened in 1912, it was an astonishing achievement. The shame is that only one of them lasted beyond 1934, but it was a vastly changed world by then. In the cold light of day, though, it would be very difficult to make a financial case for building any of them and these were the ones that got passed!

The second network lines were built to a tighter budget as can be seen in the plainer buildings, though in terms of facilities they were just the same.

The timetable for the Plouescat to Rosporden line which was treated as one route, a whopping 137km long. That's asking a lot of a Corpet Louvet tank.

Not all the trains traversed the whole route, understandably, but if you wanted to do so you could leave Plouescat at 6.10 in the morning and arrive in Rosporden at quarter past four! Bearing in mind that other than in first class the coaches had hard wooden seats, that would be quite an endurance test.

The line wasn't built with through travel in mind, of course; most journeys would have been short and only one train each way did the whole route in one go. The timetable was not exactly intensive, most stations only having three services in each direction per day, but no doubt that was sufficient.

To take a shorter journey as an example, from Plouescat to Landivisiau Ville was 24km and took one hour and twenty three minutes with three stops on the way. That's a pretty slow average speed of just over 17km per hour or 10mph which was fine as long as there was no competition.

LOCOMOTIVES AND ROLLING STOCK.

STEAM LOCOMOTIVES

The first locomotive to be acquired was built by Amédée Bollée in 1892. An 0-4-0 vertical boilered tram locomotive, it carried the number 1 and was named Brest.

Locomotives 1 to 29 were all Corpet Louvet 0-6-0 tanks, none of which carried names other than number 29 'PORSPDER' although names were allocated to all of them. They were built for the opening of the first lines in 1892 and were delivered from that date in three batches, Nos 1-7, then 8-12 and finally 13 to 29. The earliest loco's were 15 tons but the later ones were 17 tons.

Confusingly it seems that the vertical boilered loco and the first Corpet Louvet both carried the number 1, but the former was only used around the yard at Brest and was very quickly withdrawn having proved to be of limited value.

RAILCARS

In 1922 trials were undertaken with railbuses between Plouescat and Rosporden which was the longest single run on the system. As a result of the trials three railcars and three trailers were purchased initially and later more railbuses were added to the fleet. The railbuses came from three different manufacturers:

GMC/Baert & Verney Eleven railcars were constructed on a GMC 2 ton truck chassis by Baert & Verney at Le Mans. These railcars were powered by a 22 hp engine and seated 24 passengers with an additional 16 standing. They were single ended and had to be turned on a turntable at the end of their journey. Single axle trailers were hauled which seated another 20 people.

Panhard These 8 railcars had an 80 hp engine and seated 32 people. They were introduced in 1930.

Brissoneau & Lotz Obtained from the CdF Charentes this single railcar was powered by a 135 hp diesel engine with electric transmission. It carried 52 people plus a baggage compartment but was little used and passed to the Cote du Nord in 1947.

Although the railcars reduced costs they were unable to reverse the downward trend in the passenger numbers which lead to the inevitable closures.

The CFDF loco's and stock were maintained at Brest.

LOCO'S FOR THE SECOND NETWORK

When the CFA network was built from 1912 further steam locomotives were ordered, as follows:

15 Corpet-Louvet 0-6-0T locomotives, numbered 101 to 115. These were slightly heavier at 17.5 tons.

1 Blanc-Misseron 0-6-0T locomotive.

Around 1930, a single railbus was ordered from De Dion-Bouton.

The CFA loco's and stock were maintained at Chateauneuf station.

One of the first batch of railcars from Baert and Verney, number 5, with the two wheeled trailer which looks as though it would have given a very uncomfortable ride. Note the brass bell mounted on the radiator.

The livery was probably red and cream.

Corpet Louvet number 6, from the first batch of 1892. The buffer beam is lettered 'F' on the left with the number on the right.

Number 12 is differently lettered and there is lining visible on the buffer beam. The item in front of the side tank is a re-railing jack.

This loco does not have a Westinghouse pump, so presumably it is an early picture and they were fitted after the loco's had entered service. It certainly looks better without the air reservoirs on both sidetanks.

One of the later Corpet Louvet engines showing the different style of cab roof.

A superb side view of one of the later engines with the overall cab roof and the more modern looking smokebox door. The loco has Stephenson valve gear. The cylindrical tank on the side tank is an air reservoir for the braking system.

Number 106 was one of the engines bought in 1912 for the opening of the various new lines of the CFA. The air pump for the Westinghouse brakes is on the front of the right hand side tank.

Although these engines were slightly heavier they were pretty much identical to the later CFDF loco's.

No. 23, one of the last batch of CFDF engines.

Number 17, another of the last batch in the CFDF fleet.

This view shows plates on the tankside which are not present on the others so it may be the sole example that carried it's name, number 29 'Porspoder'. The makers plate is on the cabside. The open backed cab is clear; as there were ample turntables engines were run facing forwards whenever possible.

Studying all the black and white images of these railways can leave you with the impression that they were colourless places but nothing could be further from the truth. No information seems to have survived about the colour scheme used on the steam loco's but the preserved Corpet Louvet No 75 at least gives us an impression of how colourful the little Finistere trains must have been.

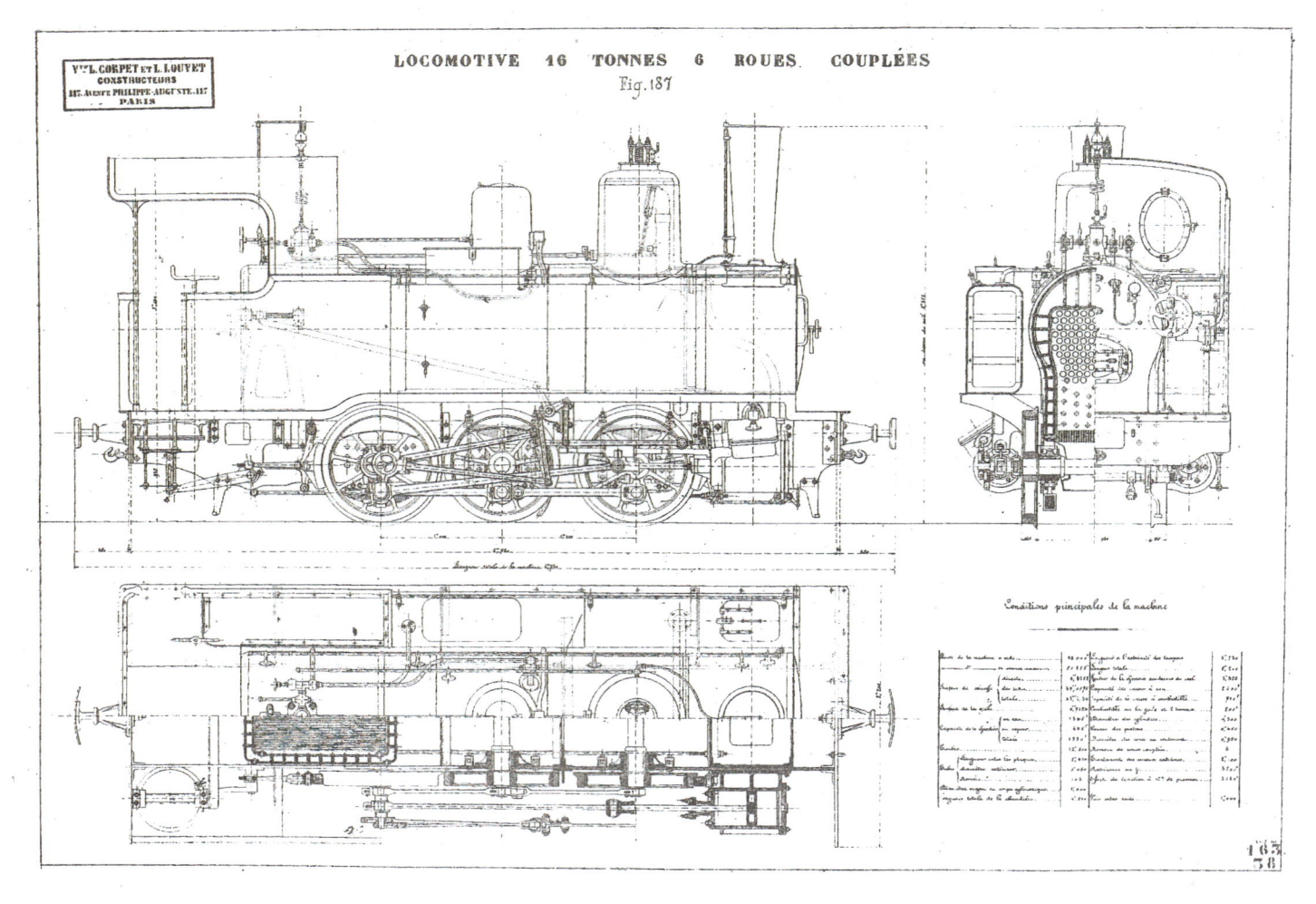

PASSENGER COACHING STOCK:

The company bought a total of 132 coaches, mainly from Blanc Misseron and ANF but also from Carel, Fouche and Decauville in smaller numbers.

FOUR WHEELED COACHES:

There was a single lounge coach, perhaps used by the directors or possibly hired out to parties.

Eleven first class coaches numbered A1 to A11 with seating for 16 people and room for another 6 to stand.

Forty similar second class coaches numbered B1 to B30 and B61 to B70.

Fifteen similar second class coaches with two compartments, numbered BB1 to BB8, Bb46 to Bb509 and BB71 and 72

BOGIE COACHES:

Twenty six second class coaches numbered Bx31 to Bx45 and Bx51 to Bx61.

Fourteen 1st/2nd class composite coaches numbered AB1 to AB10 and BA1 to BA4.

Ten open coaches used only in the summer, numbered C1 to C10….known as 'rug hookers' apparently!

FOURGONS:

Fifteen vans, numbered D1 to D15.

FREIGHT STOCK:

82 K series vans, 37 of them with Westinghouse brakes.

39 H series tipper wagons, 18 of them with Westinghouse brakes.

17 L series tipper wagons, 6 of them with Westinghouse brakes.

60 M series dropside open wagons, 26 of them with Westinghouse brakes.

10 bogie bolster wagons.

2 breakdown wagons.

Additional goods stock was purchased in 1912:

48 J series covered vans, 19 of them with Westinghouse brakes.

38 K series tarpaulin wagons.

32 L series open wagons.

20 M series dropside open wagons.

14 N series open wagons.

6 P series flat wagons.

The livery of the coaching stock has passed unrecorded but they were certainly painted rather than varnished wood. My guess would be dark green with yellow or cream lettering, but we'll probably never know for sure.

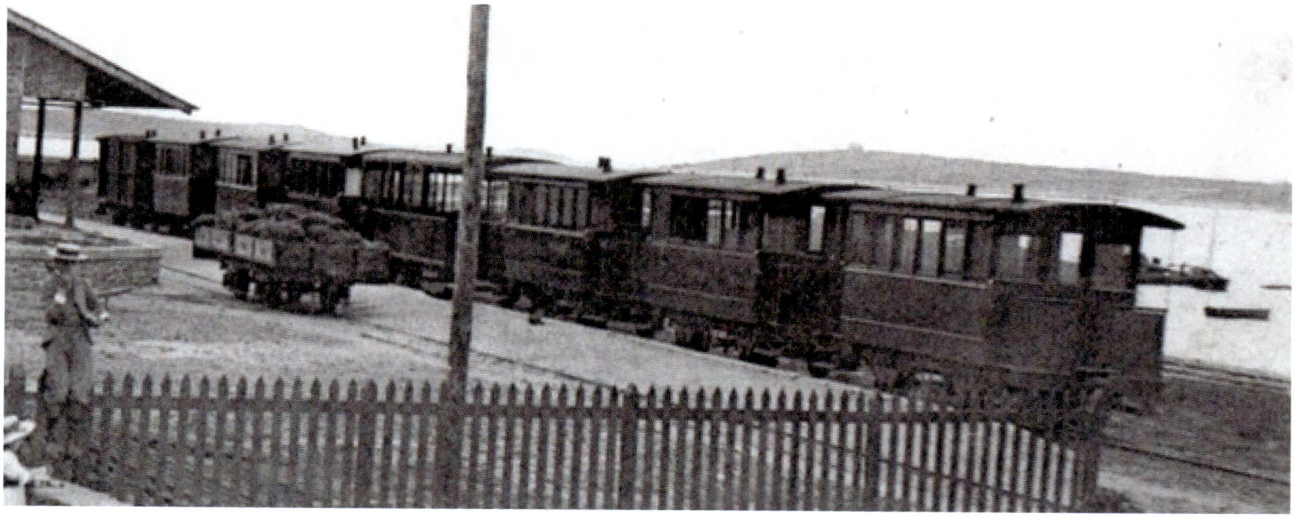

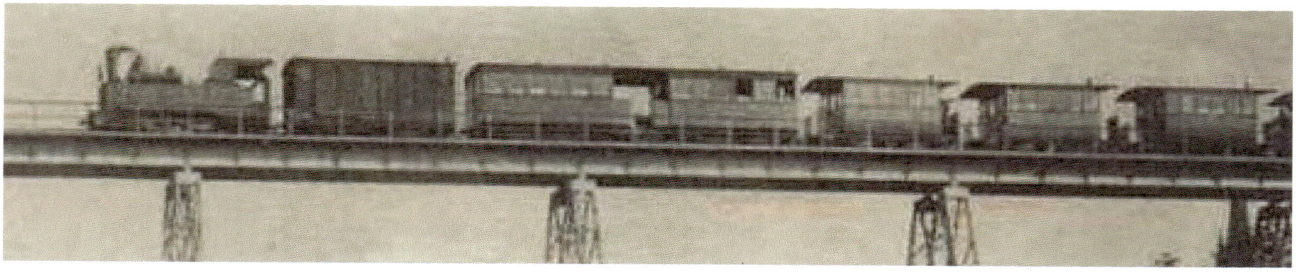

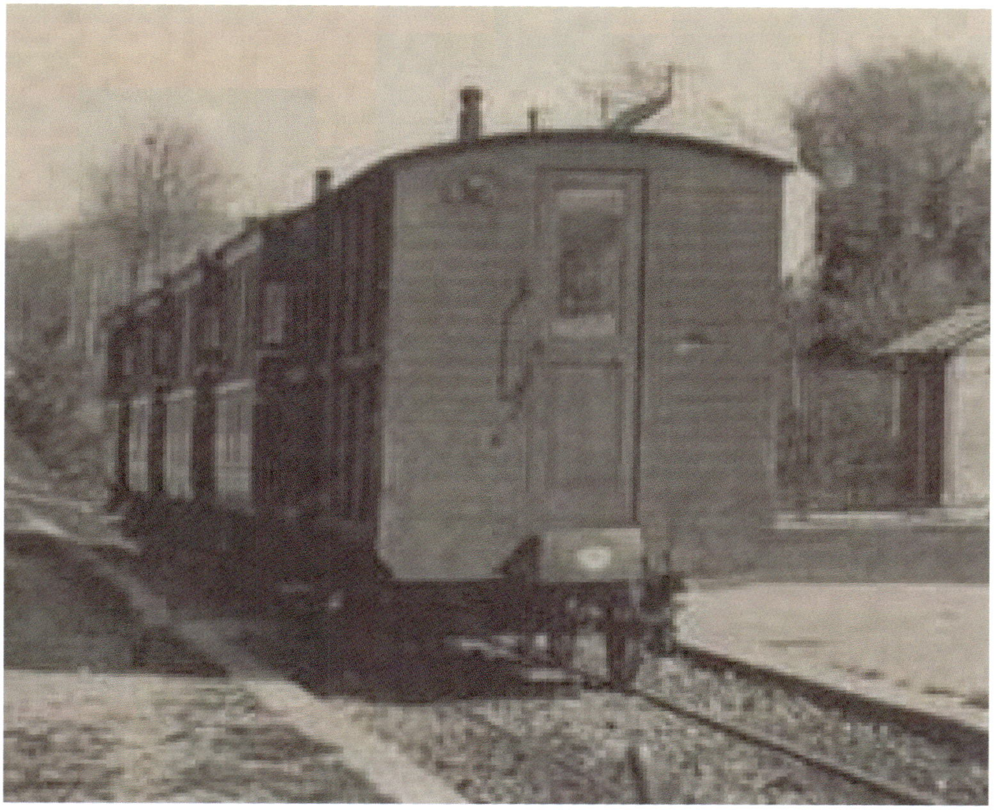

An enlargement of one of the Fourgons; it seems to have a veranda at each end and looks to be open at the ends above waist level.

The side doors slide over the outside framing. Note also the unusual W irons which are outside the axle boxes.

These are extremely unusual vehicles, unlike any I have seen elsewhere.

The one below is totally different so there must have been at least two batches unless one is CFDF and one is CFA. However, they were both pictured at Porspoder station.

Good pictures of the other goods stock are elusive—this is the best I can do.

NORTHERN FINISTERE.

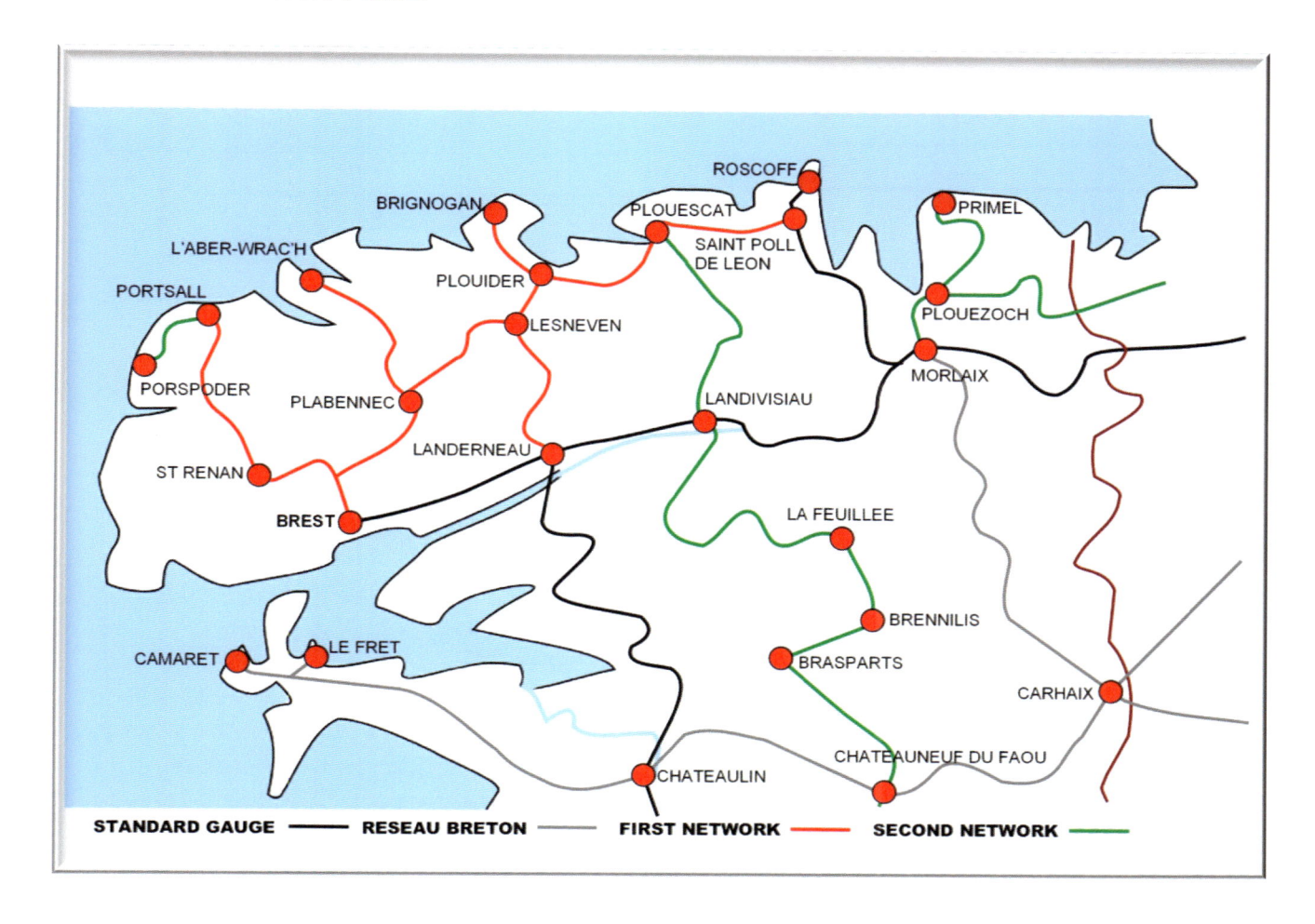

FIRST NETWORK.

1. BREST TO PORTSALL
2. BREST TO L'ABER-WRAC'H
3. PLABENNEC TO LESNEVEN
4. LANDERNEAU RO BRIGNOGAN
5. PLOUIDER TO PLOUESCAT AND ST POL.

SECOND NETWORK

1. CHATEAUNEUF DU FAOU TO LANDIVISIAU AND PLOUESCAT
2. MORLAIX TO PRIMEL.
3. PORTSALL TO PORSPODER.

BREST TO PORTSALL & PORSPODER

BREST STATION

LOCOMOTIVE SHED

GOODS SHED

STATION BUILDING

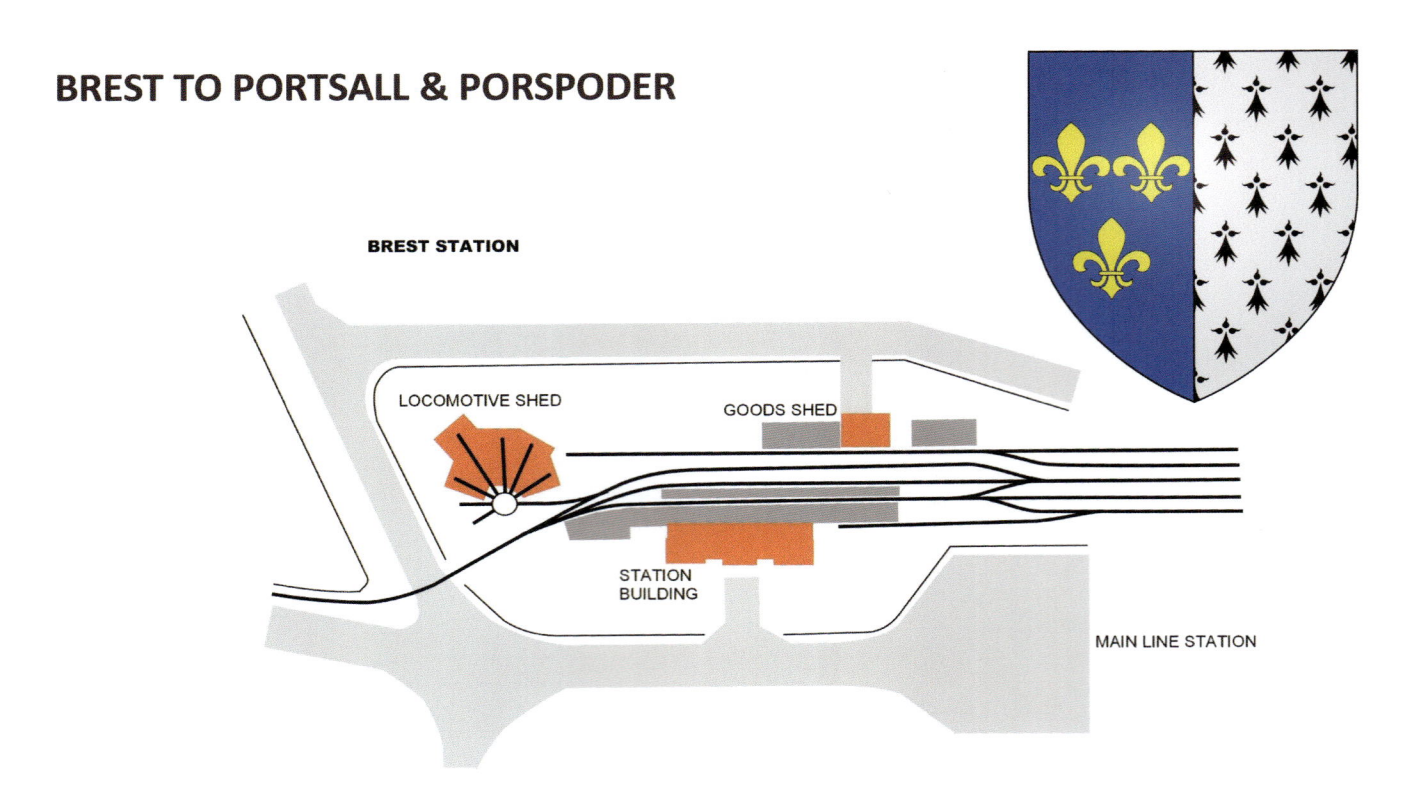

MAIN LINE STATION

The first narrow gauge line from Brest ran to the coast at Ploudalmezeau and opened on May 14th 1893 as far as St Renan and beyond there on July 14th which appropriately was Bastille Day. The CdF du Finistere line terminated just outside the impressive Ouest station, so not be outdone the CFDF built an opulent station themselves, at least on the road approach side. The track plan was pretty much standard narrow gauge with three loops and the loco shed was very close by, but the point had been made. Lines continued beyond the station to run alongside the standard gauge in order to facilitate the transfer of goods.

Unfortunately the postcard publishers seem to have been so awestruck by the new station that they forgot to walk around the other side to photograph the interesting part, all the pictures showing the approach road side.

3387. - BREST. - La Gare des Chemins de Fer Départementaux

Collection H. Laurent, Port-Louis

The station was absolutely superb, and presumably must have housed the company offices on the upper floors. The last trains ran in 1946 and sadly the site was cleared in 1950 to make way for a bus station.

Below, a CFDF train runs away from the station along the roadside, with the Ouest station in the background. The line on the right is the electric town tramway which ran from 1903 until 1932.

Just north of Brest the line crossed this impressive viaduct at Lamezellec, which is now a suburb of Brest.

SAINT RENAN

41. SAINT-RENAN (Finistère) — Place de la Gare

The line to Plouennec diverged at Guilers and the first station on the Portsall line served St Renan, a town of two thousand people when the line opened. The station here pretty much established the standard pattern for all the first network routes. The attractive station building included accommodation for the station master, and by it stood a wooden goods shed with a wide awning on both sides protecting the loading doors. A stone faced loading platform extended beyond the goods shed alongside which a siding ran from a wagon turntable. The two tracks of the loop ran on either side of a low platform, earth surfaced.

St-RENAN - La Gare ... Collection E. Le Bihan (49)

Renan station—the upper picture may show the opening day as such crowds would not have been seen in normal circumstances. The station wasn't a crossing place for passengers trains, so near to Brest that was not necessary.

PLOUDALMEZEAU

This was the terminus of the line from 1893 until the extension to Portsall opened on July 14th 1899. The town today has a population of six thousand.

PLOUDALMÉZEAU. – La Gare avant l'Arrivée d'un Train.

The station had the same design of symmetrical station building, with the goods shed here on the right and the little toilet block on the left.

Ploudalmézeau – Gare

Between Ploualmezeau and Portsall was the viaduct at Kersaint which still stands today.

PORTSALL

Although the station was separate Portsall is considered to be part of Ploudalmezeau.

This was the termnius from the line opening on July 14th 1899 until on May 13th 1913 the extension to Porspoder was opened as part of the second network under the CFA.

The station followed exactly the same pattern as has been seen previously; the surfaced and edged platform in front of the station building was an unusual feature not often seen on narrow gauge lines in France. Between the tracks is the usual beaten earth surface.

123 PORTSALL. – La Gare

PORTSALL STATION

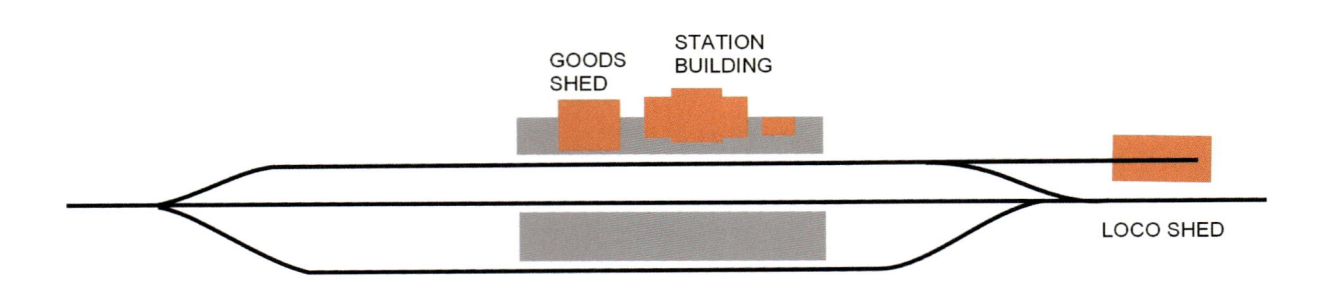

GOODS SHED — STATION BUILDING — LOCO SHED

The locomotive shed would have been required when the station was a terminus. When the line was extended no alterations were made to the track plan, it was perfectly adequate for the traffic on offer.

This are good views of the road side of the standard buildings.

PORSPODER

This was the terminus of the line from Brest until closure in 1935. With 1821 inhabitants in 1906 it isn't a large enough place to have generated much traffic for the railway, certainly outside the holiday season.

Having been built later, the architecture here was different with a much smaller station building. With a loco shed being built here it may well be that the one at Portsall went out of use when the extension opened; there would have been no need for both to remain open. This is an excellent view of one of the outside frames Fourgons.

PORSPODOR STATION

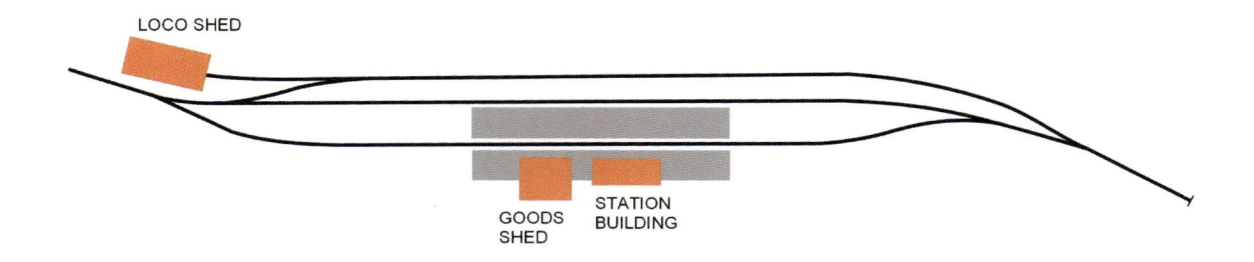

The gable roofed structure is the goods shed, the station building has a flat roof and stands to the left of it. This was quite an exposed spot close to the coast, very bleak in the winter. Terminus stations don't get much more minimal than this.

450 — PORSPODER (Finistère). La Gare.   ND. Phot.

This is a good view of one of the railway's covered vans. The passenger train has three bogie coaches and a four wheeler bringing up the rear, but there is no Fourgon.

PORSPODER — La Gare

BREST TO L'ABER-WRAC'H

PLABENNEC Plabennec is the first station on the line north from Brest to L'Aber-wac'h on the coast which opened on February 26th 1904 and it became the junction for Plouider on July 11th 1904. The town had 3836 people in 1906.

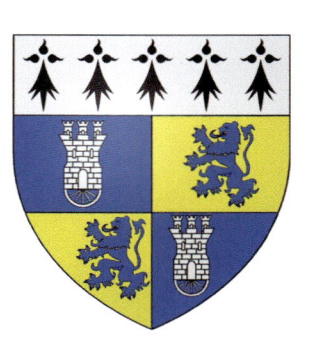

The standard buildings from the first network are seen again here, and there are four loops to allow trains to pass and connecting services to wait. Three water towers seems a little excessive!

LANNILLIS

The next station was at Lannillis, a town of three and a half thousand people in 1906.

The station followed the same pattern, with just one loop so it was not a passing place. The outside framed Fourgon is interesting.

Lannilis. — La Gare, le départ du train

One of the staff seems to have been a keen gardener.

In the lower picture baskets of fruit or vegetables await loading into the Fourgon.

L. P.   133   LANNILIS. — La Gare. — Arrivée du Train.

Not crossed by the railway but interesting none the less was this lovely suspension bridge which opened in 1851. Sadly it was replaced by a very much less attractive girder bridge in 1933. The French generally have a flair for bridges, but in 1933 it deserted them!

L'ABER-WRAC'H

The terminus of the line was at L'Aber-wrac'h, on the north coast. The name of the town derives from a rock in the river where it meets the sea called the 'Old woman'.

The line beyond Lannilis opened on Febraury 25th 1900 and closed in 1932.

The station was in a delightful position right by the river though it must have been a bit windswept at times right on the north coast. The standard architecture is seen again which did the job perfectly well.

The station building survives and is in excellent condition as the local tourist office.

L'ABER-VRACH – La Gare

An early railcar receives some attention, something that no doubt happened all the time. Behind it can be seen the roof of the locomotive shed which was accessed via a turntable.

3248. L'ABERWRACH — Les Quais de la Gare

The building in the distance is the lifeboat station, which the railway ran alongside.

A wagon turntable allowed wagons to be shunted onto a short siding alongside the loading platform; in the lower picture a van can be seen alongside the goods shed.

Laberwrac'h (Finistère). — La Gare

L'Aber-Wrach — Gare construite sur le Quai

PLABENNEC TO LESNEVEN

This short section of line opened on February 14th 1904, connecting the line to L'Aber-wrac'h with that to Brignogan and Plouescat. It closed in 1946.

There were no intermediate stations.

LANDERNEAU TO BRIGNOGAN

This line was opened in two stages, from Landereau to Plouneour on June 11th 1894 and from Plouneour to Brignonan on August 11th 1901, both as part of the first network. Plouneour is only just outside Brignogan so the extension was only 2km long.

LANDERNEAU

Landerneau had a station on the Ouest main line to Brest and it was from here that the CFDF line began. The town had around eight thousand inhabitants when the line opened so it was a good source of revenue. The coat of arms is superb, but odd in that this isn't a coastal town.

Unfortunately pictures of the narrow gauge here do not seem to exist.

LESNEVEN The first station north of Landerneau was at Lesneven which became the junction for Plabennec in 1904, ten years after the station opened. The town had three and a half thousand people when the line opened.

The standard architecture was used again, of course.

After it became a junction the station was enlarged with four loops to give room for trains to stand and pass.

L. P., Brest 52. LESNEVEN. — La Gare, un jour de marché, à l'arrivée de trois trains

Presumably the factory on the right would have contributed traffic. Four trains at one time must have tested the staff to the utmost, just making sure everyone got on the correct one!

The lower picture reveals that there is an engine shed, probably added in 1904.

Lesneven. — La Gare

PLOUIDER The next station along the line was at Plouider which also became a junction when the line to Plouescat was opened on July 11th 1904. Plouider is only a village, with under two thousand people today.

The station looks rather different with a much smaller twin pavilion station building built in the same style as the larger structures.

The is a single loop with sidings fed from a wagon turntable, but there does not seem to have been a goods shed.

The station building has survived, though it does not look well cared for.

PLOUNEOUR-TREZ

This was the end of the line from the opening on June 11th 1894 until August 11th 1901 when the 2km long extension to Brignogan was opened. With a population of only around a thousand it was certainly not the reason for building the line which was always intended to serve Brignogan.

I cannot find any pictures of the station in use, but the main building survives as a house in very nice condition.

BRIGNOGAN

The surprise comes when you discover that Brignogan has even fewer people, only around 800 when the line was built. It must have been intended to tap into the holiday traffic, indeed the village now calls itself Brignogan Plage.

Again there was a small station building, in a different style to those already used.

436 — BRIGNOGAN (Finistère). La Gare: Arrivée du Train. ND Phot.

This picture enables one to deuce that there were three loops, with a loading platform for goods but no goods shed. Freight traffic would have been minimal. This is a good view of loco number 6.

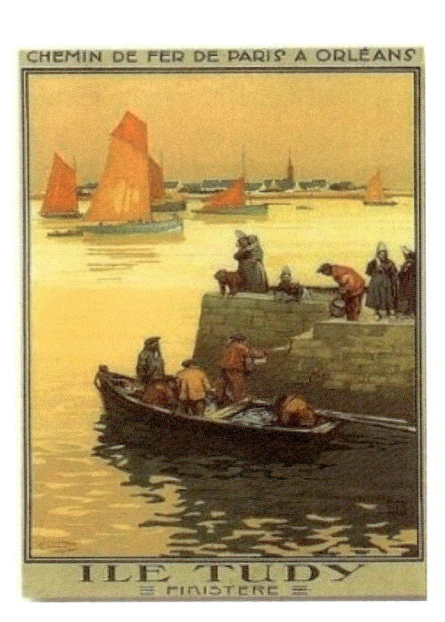

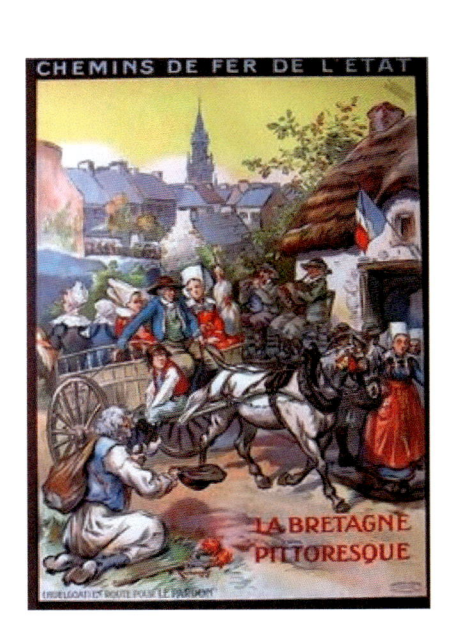

PLOUIDER TO PLOUESCAT AND ST POL DE LEON.

This line ran along the north coast and was opened on July 11th 1904 to Plouescat and on 1st July 1907 to St Pol which was a station on the Ouest branch to Roscoff.

PLOUESCAT   Plouescat is a town of nearly four thousand people today and so was a valuable source of traffic for the railway.

Here for some reason a totally different style of main building was used, though still with the separate wooden goods shed with an overhanging roof. There are four loops as seen before at the junction stations, a line running south from Plouecat to Landivisiau which opened on November 10th 1912. The main building may date from then, replacing an earlier smaller structure.

This seems to have been the only picture taken of the station.

SAINT POL DE LEON

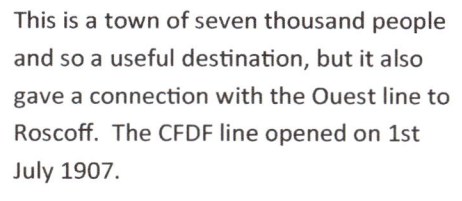

This is a town of seven thousand people and so a useful destination, but it also gave a connection with the Ouest line to Roscoff. The CFDF line opened on 1st July 1907.

SAINT-POL-DE-LEON (Finistère). — Vue intérieure de la Gare. ND. Phot.

Sadly all the pictures I have show the Ouest station and not the narrow gauge.

SAINT-POL-de-LÉON. - La Gare, vue intérieure

PLOUESCAT TO LANDIVISIAU

LANDIVISIAU This section of line opened on November 10th 1912, and so was part of the second network. Landivisiau is a station on the Ouest main line serving a town of nearly five thousand people in 1906.

19 - LANDIVISIAU. — Vue générale de la Gare

The building in the foreground is the CFA station which was separate from the Ouest yet conveniently placed for the transfer of traffic. The station building still exists, another of the plainer buildings used on the CFA lines.

LANDIVISIAU. — Les Gares, vue d'ensemble

This picture clearly shows the relationship between the two stations. The water tower is under construction.

A CFA goods train crossing the Ouest station approach road.

LANDIVISIAU (Finistère). — La Gare

There was a separate CFA station at Landivisiau Ville, with a larger station building and goods shed and on the left a single tracked engine shed. The loco below is No. 113.

20 LANDIVISIAU — Gares de l'Etat et du C.-F.-A.

Above is the terminus at the Ouest station and below is the Ville station with the town behind it.

LANDIVISIAU — Vue d'ensemble

LANDIVISIAU TO ROSPORDEN

A second line was opened from Landivisiau in stages during 1912. It ran due south to Rosporden station on the PO Railway, connecting several villages en-route. The line only lasted until 1933 and should certainly never have been built but that's with the benefit of hindsight; no one in 1912 know that the First World War was going to take place and the effects it would have on life in the 1920's and 1930's.

The line made an end on connection with the existing route and thereafter the line was operated as one.

This chapter will describe the line as far south as Chateauneuf du Faou, with the remainder being covered in the following section.

The first station was at Commana but no pictures of it have surfaced to date.

LA FEUILLEE

No one was going to get rich building a railway to here, with only 600 inhabitants as potential customers.

La Feuillee pictured when it was brand new. The section to here opened on June 11th 1912, and the next section to the south on November 25th so in the interim this was a terminus which may explain the need for a loco shed. The gable roofed station design has been used again, but there is also an attractive goods shed with an overhanging roof. The picture may even pre-date the opening, it all looks spotless.

LA FEUILLEE STATION

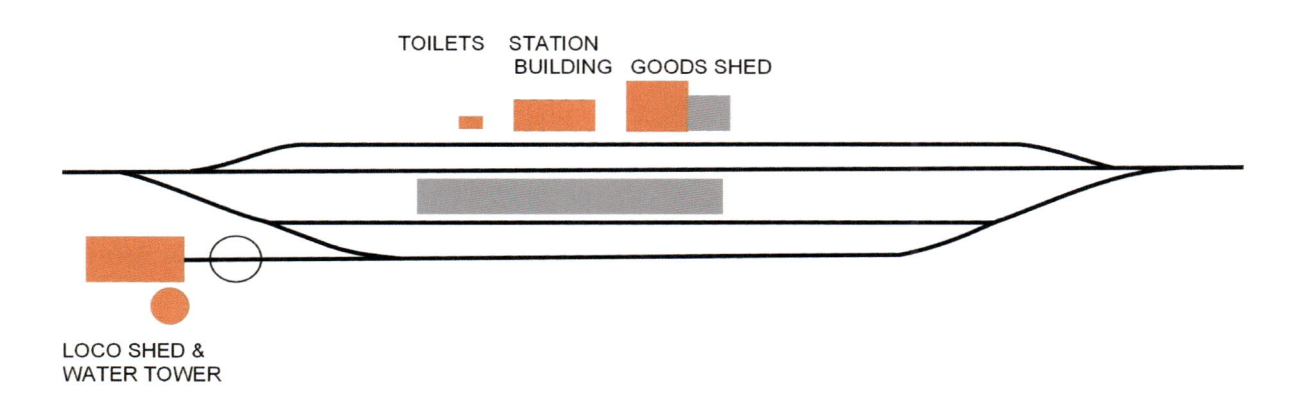

TOILETS STATION BUILDING GOODS SHED

LOCO SHED & WATER TOWER

This looks to have been taken during the construction of the line in 1911 or 1912.

65

The next station to the south served the little village of Brasparts, but no pictures have been found. The line opened from here through to Chateauneuf du Faou on November 25th 1912.

CHATEAUNEUF DU FAOU

At Chateauneuf the line crossed the Reseau Breton and there were adjacent stations, but although they were both metre gauge there was no physical connection. The CFA workshops were here, with repair shops and a paint shop as well as a loco shed. The town had four thousand people in 1906 so it was a sensible place to base the repair shops with a potential workforce on hand.

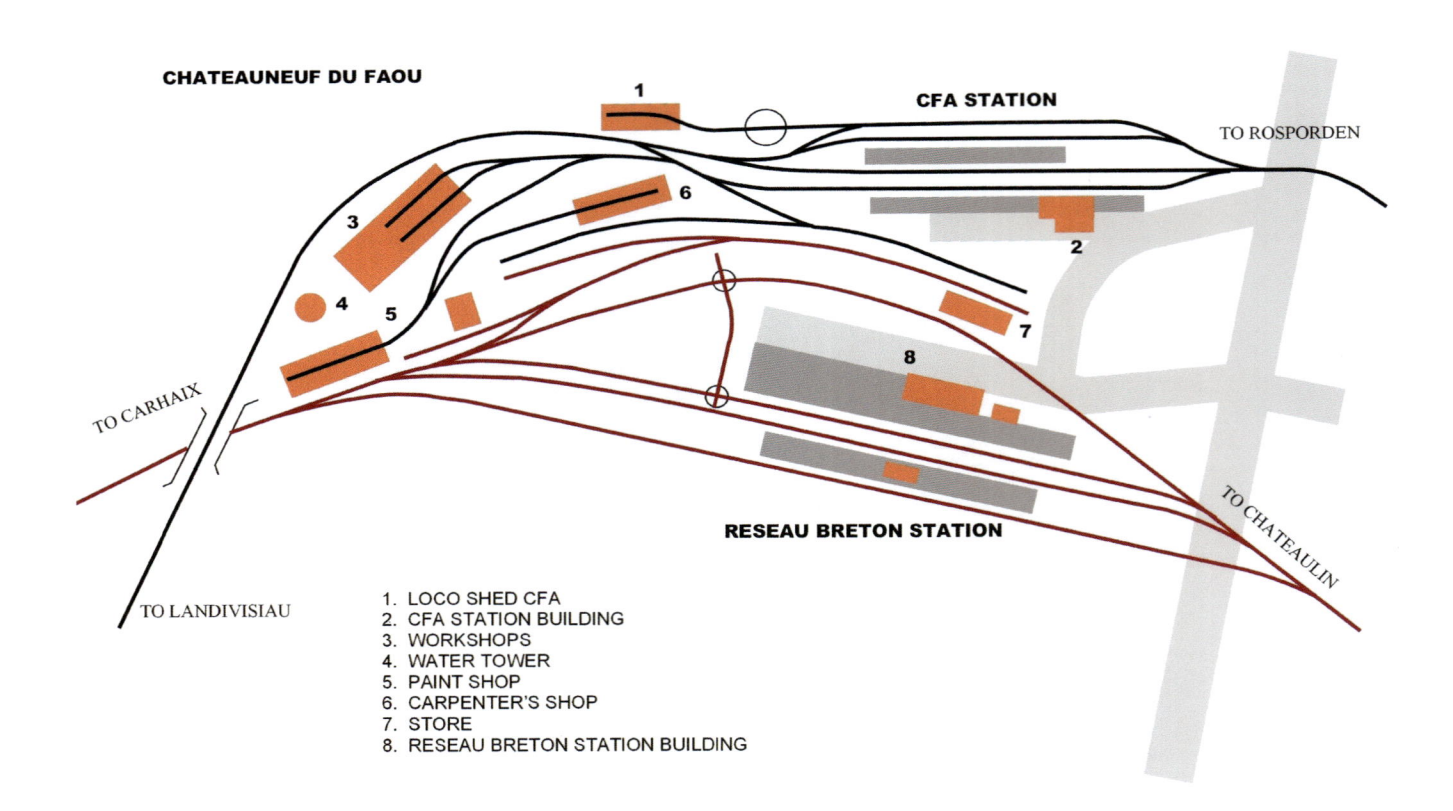

1. LOCO SHED CFA
2. CFA STATION BUILDING
3. WORKSHOPS
4. WATER TOWER
5. PAINT SHOP
6. CARPENTER'S SHOP
7. STORE
8. RESEAU BRETON STATION BUILDING

The Reseau Breton station closed to all traffic in 1967 with the line to Camaret, though the station building survives.

Châteauneuf-du-Faou. — La Gare

This is the Reseau Breton station, probably before the CFA line had been built. The RB station remained pretty much unaltered, the CFA curving around it and then crossing the RB on a bridge. The CFA station would be on the right behind the station building.

Another picture almost certainly taken before 1912.

6715. - CHATEAUNEUF du-FAOU. - La Gare

I have been unable to find any pictures showing the CFA station or workshops, but happily the station building does survive showing that it was built to the usual second network design in local stone with a gabled roof.

The goods shed can be seen beyond the station, in the usual manner. The house beyond the station has been built on the trackbed of the CFA since the line closed in 1933. The remaining CFA buildings on the site have been demolished.

MORLAIX TO PRIMEL AND PLESTIN LES GREVES.

The final line to be described in this section ran north from Morlaix, where it made an end on connection with the Reseau Breton. It ran to the coastal town of Primel and opened as part of the second network on 1st May 1912. A branch opened on 1st March 1913 which left the line at Plouezoc'h and ran to Pont Menou; it was then extended to Plestin les Greves where it made a connection with the Cote du Nord system which opened to Plestin in 1916. The CFA line to Plestin closed in 1932 and the main branch closed in 1934.

PRIMEL   Primel is a tiny community on the north coast of Finistere where the railway terminated. The line ran this far purely to accommodate the holiday traffic, the town of Plougasnou being 1km inland.

The little terminus had the usual second network station building with a small goods shed attached to it. Here Corpet Louvet No 106 waits to leave with two coaches and a Fourgon.

PLOUGASNOU The town of Plougasnou had a population of nearly four thousand when the line opened so this was the main reason for building it rather than traffic to Primel.

1900 PLOUGASNOU (Finistère). — La Gare et l'Entrée du Bourg.

The usual arrangement of a second network station was repeated here with the buildings constructed in attractive local stone. The church marks the town centre so it was a good walk from the station.

11940 — PLOUGASNOU (Finistère) — La Gare   ES.

PLOUEZOC'H

This was the junction station for Plestin and the Cote du Nord system. With a population today of sixteen hundred it was more important as a junction than as a source of traffic in it's own right.

11939 - PLOUEZOC'H (Finistère) — La Gare

The buildings are again to the standard pattern, but as befits a junction there are four loop lines to allow trains to pass and to reverse. This picture looks to have been taken very soon after the station opened.

The station is the building in the middle distance in the lower picture.

PLOUEZOCH - St-Antoine — Quartier de la Gare

LANMEUR

On the 1913 branch to Plestin, Lanmeur is a town of just over two thousand people today.

LANMEUR - La Gare

The station was laid out in the standard pattern, again with stone built buildings. One loop was sufficient as this wasn't a passing place for passenger trains.

1796 — LANMEUR (Finistère). La Gare. ND. Phot.

PLESTIN LES GREVES

The station at Plestin les Greves was built and owned by the CdF Cote du Nord and opened in 1916 in part to give the CdN system a route to the port of Morlaix through which munitions could be imported. The CFA line had opened in 1913 as far as Pont Menou. After World War One the line became very much a backwater and it closed in 1932, the first part of the CFA to do so.

A 1920's picture of a CFA train at the tiny station built by the Cote du Nord company at Plestin les Greves.

A good number of passengers seem to be using the service, perhaps for a special occasion of some sort which is why the picture was taken.

MORLAIX

Morlaix is by far the largest town in this area and it was the natural place for the narrow gauge to begin. The population was nearly sixteen thousand in 1906. The town was already served by the Ouest and the Reseau Breton, but the CFA was the line to the seaside!

1491 MORLAIX. - Le Quai de Tréguier et ... - N...

The town is dominated by the magnificent viaduct on the Ouest line to Brest, which the Reseau Breton also ran across using a third rail as they shared the facilities at the Ouest station. The CFA was a little more self effacing, trundling along the river bank as seen here.

1492 MORLAIX. — Le Bassin et la Manufacture des Tabacs. ND. Phot.

74

The CFA ran beneath the viaduct and had a station there which was conveniently placed for the town centre.

The caption below reads 'the railway from Morlaix to the sea'!

1430 MORLAIX (Finistère). ND. Phot.
Le Viaduc et la Nouvelle Ligne des Chemins de Fer Armoricains.

55 MORLAIX. — Gare du Chemin de Fer de Morlaix à la Mer. — LL

4 MORLAIX — Vue d'ensemble du Viaduc (haut. 58 m., long. 202 m.) — ND

1500 — MORLAIX. Statue du Corsaire Cornic et le Bassin. ND Phot.

MORLAIX. Le Port et le Cours Beaumont

1730 — MORLAIX (Finistère). Le Square et la Gare du Styvel.   ND.

North of the viaduct and the town centre was Styvel station which seems to have been the Morlaix goods station for the CFA.

There is a passing loop in the lower picture so presumably it was also a stopping place.

1435 — MORLAIX. Le Chemin de fer à la Maison de Paille.   ND Phot

The CFA line ran alongside the river for a considerable distance as it left Morlaix; it must have been a very attractive ride.

A tributary of the River Morlaix was crossed at Dourduff, about 4km beyond Morlaix.

120 MORLAIX. — Pont sur le Dourduff. — LL.

1400 - Environs de MORLAIX. Le Pont de Dourduff. ND Phot.

113 MORLAIX. — Le Chemin de Fer armoricain au Dourduff. — LL.

SOUTHERN FINISTERE

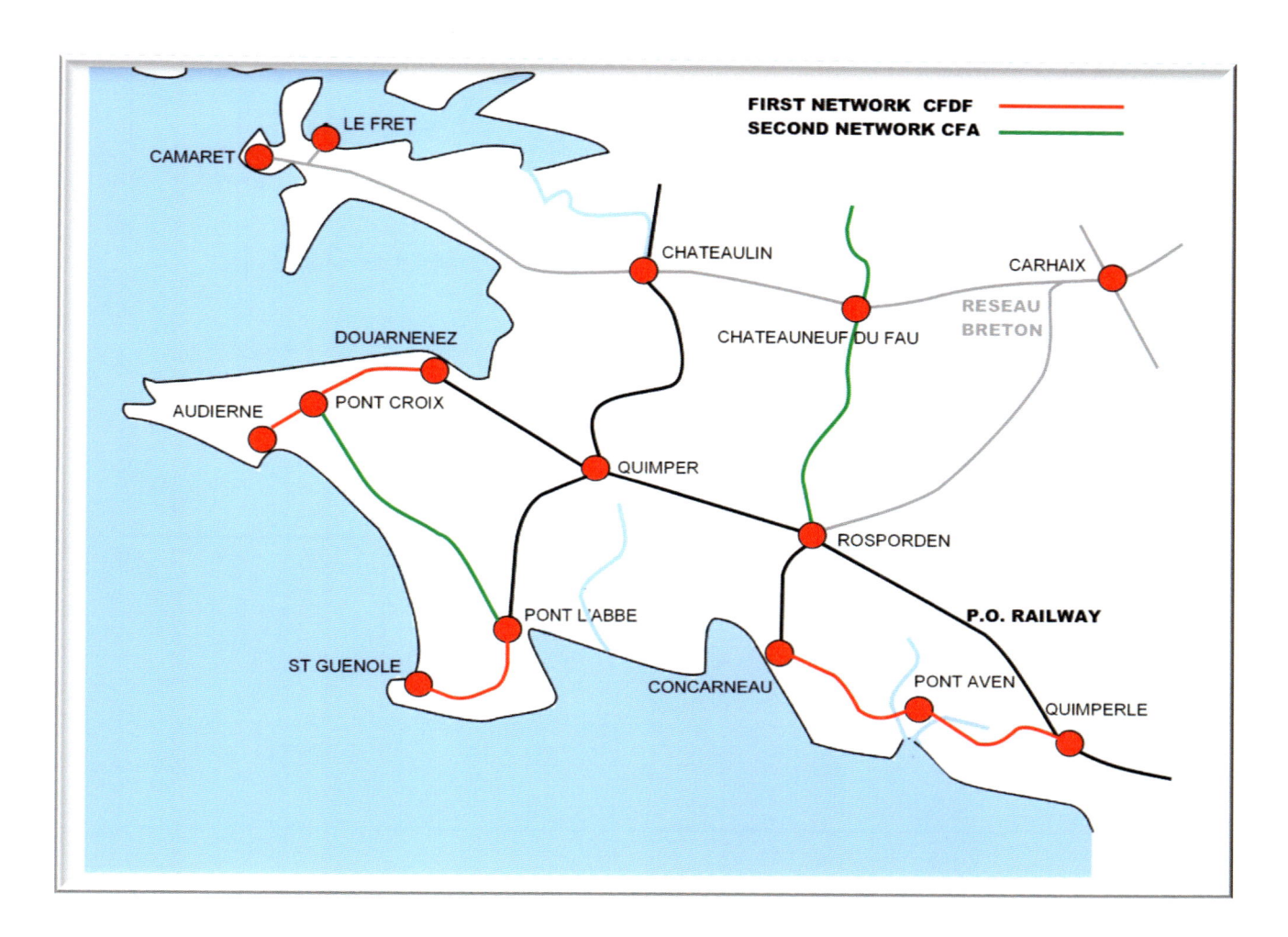

FIRST NETWORK

1. DOUARNENEZ TO AUDIERNE
2. PONT L'ABBE TO ST GUENOLE
3. CONCARNEAU TO QUIMPERLE

SECOND NETWORK

1. PONT CROIX TO PONT L'ABBE
2. ROSPORDEN TO CHATEAUNEUF DU FOU

DOUARNENEZ TO PONT CROIX AND AUDIERNE.

Douarnenez was the terminus of a standard gauge line built by the PO Railway from Quimper which opened on April 7th 1884, mainly in order to give an outlet for the produce of the fishing fleets. The line closed to passengers in 1972 and to freight in 1988 and has been converted into a green way.

The CFDF line was opened on January 29th 1894, running west along the coast to Pont Croix and then the terminus at Audierne. The line closed in 1946.

A branch was opened from Pont Croix to Pont L'Abbe on 1st October 1912 and this section closed in 1933.

DOUARNENEZ This town of fifteen thousand people is an important fishing port and it was a logical place to begin the line to serve Audiere as the PO railway was already open.

The P.O. station stood on the left bank of the river which was spanned by an impressive bridge to give access to the town. Surprisingly no pictures of the CFDF seem to exist.

PONT CROIX

Pont Croix is a community of sixteen hundred people lying a little inland from the coast.

LA BRETAGNE — 13 PONT-CROIX — La Gare

The station developed when it became a junction in 1912 and the plan below shows it after that date but the picture shows the original arrangement. The structures are again the standard designs used on the first network lines.

PONT - CROIX STATION

AUDIERNE

The terminus of the line was at Audierne, a town of nearly four thousand people that lies right on the coast combining fishing with catering for the holiday trade.

57 AUDIERNE. — La Gare. — Arrivée du Train. — LL.

This was quite a complex terminus, especially by narrow gauge standards, with a much larger than usual goods shed and a two road loco shed. The station building was the usual design, however, clearly sufficient to cope with the expected traffic.

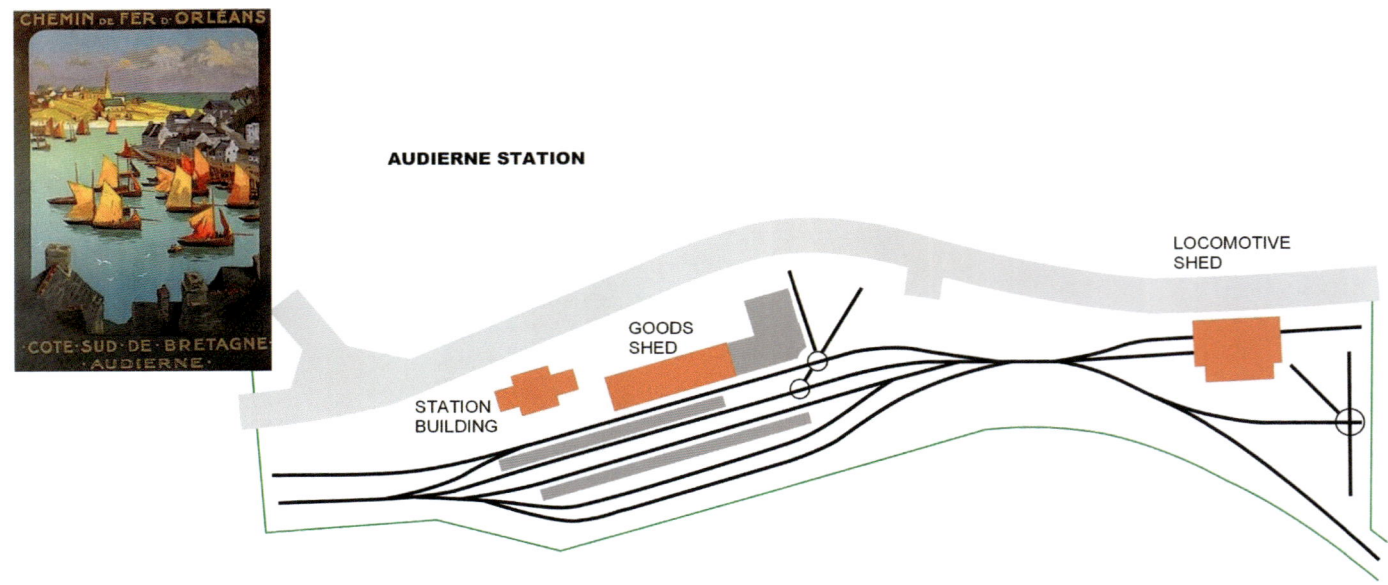

AUDIERNE STATION

3993. Audierne — Le Grand Pont du Goyen et la Gare

Collection Villard, Quimper

The station is on the right; the bridge carried road traffic, the railway terminating at the end of it. The station was in a very exposed location.

61 AUDIERNE. — La Gare. — ND Phot.

Audierne pittoresque
6. — La gare le matin à l'arrivée des touristes. (effet de contre-jour)

Coll. V. Giffard, Audierne-Paris

A small party of tourists have arrived at the station!

13 AUDIERNE. — Le Grand Pont et le Quartier de la Gare.

163. Audierne — Embouchure du Goyen - Le Pont de la Gare

Collection Villard, Quimper

The end of the station can be seen on the far right with a wagon on the headshunt.

173. De Douarnenez à Audierne — La Vallée du Goyen
La Montagne et Pont de Souganso

Collection Villard, Quimper

38 D'AUDIERNE à DOUARNENEZ.
Pont de Souganso et la Montagne. — ND Phot.

18. AUDIERNE — Le train longe la rivière de Pont-Croix à Audierne

PONT L'ABBE TO ST. GUENOLE.

This section of the system had a fascinating history. It opened on July 4th 1907 as a perfectly normal part of the first network of lines, running from Pont L'Abbe where an existing P.O. line ended which had opened in 1884. The narrow gauge line was known locally as the 'Carrots train'.

However, rather than closing with the remainder of the narrow gauge system the line to St Guenole was converted to standard gauge and connected to the P.O. line. The new standard gauge opened on May 19th 1947, the main reason for the conversion being the huge amount of fish that was being carried which all had to be transferred at Pont L'Abbe. The new line did not have any effect on the declining passenger numbers, unfortunately, and passenger trains only ran until 1950. The line remained as freight only until July 1st 1963 when it closed, the branch from Quimper to Pont L'Abbe lasting until 1988.

SAINT GUENOLE

The port lies on the exposed west facing coast and is one of four villages, Penmarch, St Guenole, Kerity and St Pierre. The community had a combined population of six thousand in 1906.

The station was extremely minimal and looks rather bleak—it's hard to imagine standard gauge trains reaching here as late as 1963, but that's what happened.

La gare de Saint-Guénolé-Penmarch

The only intermediate station of which I can find pictures is Guilvinec, a small town of nearly three thousand people, seen here with loco 114 and a group of local ladies in their distinctive costume. The goods shed looks to be a later addition.

Collection Capitaine-Ameline   1 - Guilvinec — La Gare

5577. Guilvinec — La Gare

GUILVINEC (Finistère). - Le Chemin de fer

PONT L'ABBE Pont L'Abbe was a town of six and a half thousand people in 1906 so it was well worth the P.O. building their branch to it from Quimper.

Finistère — 1030 — PONT-L'ABBÉ, la Gare

3620 PONT-L'ABBÉ — La Gare

Remarkably this is the P.O. station, in dire need of some weed killer! Sadly these postcards seem to be all there is of Pont L'Abbe, and they don't show the narrow gauge. There was a CFDF station at Pont L'Abbe Ville as well.

7125 PONT-L'ABBÉ - Vue générale de la Gare

CONCARNEAU TO QUIMPERLE

The last of the first network lines to be described ran from Concarneau, another town served by a branch of the P.O. Railway, to Quimperle by way of Pont Aven. The line was opened between Quimperle and Pont Aven on March 9th 1903, and beyond there on June 14th 1908 making Pont Aven a terminus for five years. The route closed in 1936.

CONCARNEAU

The coastal town of Concarneau is large, with over twenty thousand inhabitants today. The branch from the P.O. at Rosporden opened on June 30th 1883 and lost it's passenger service in 1959. Part of it remains open for freight.

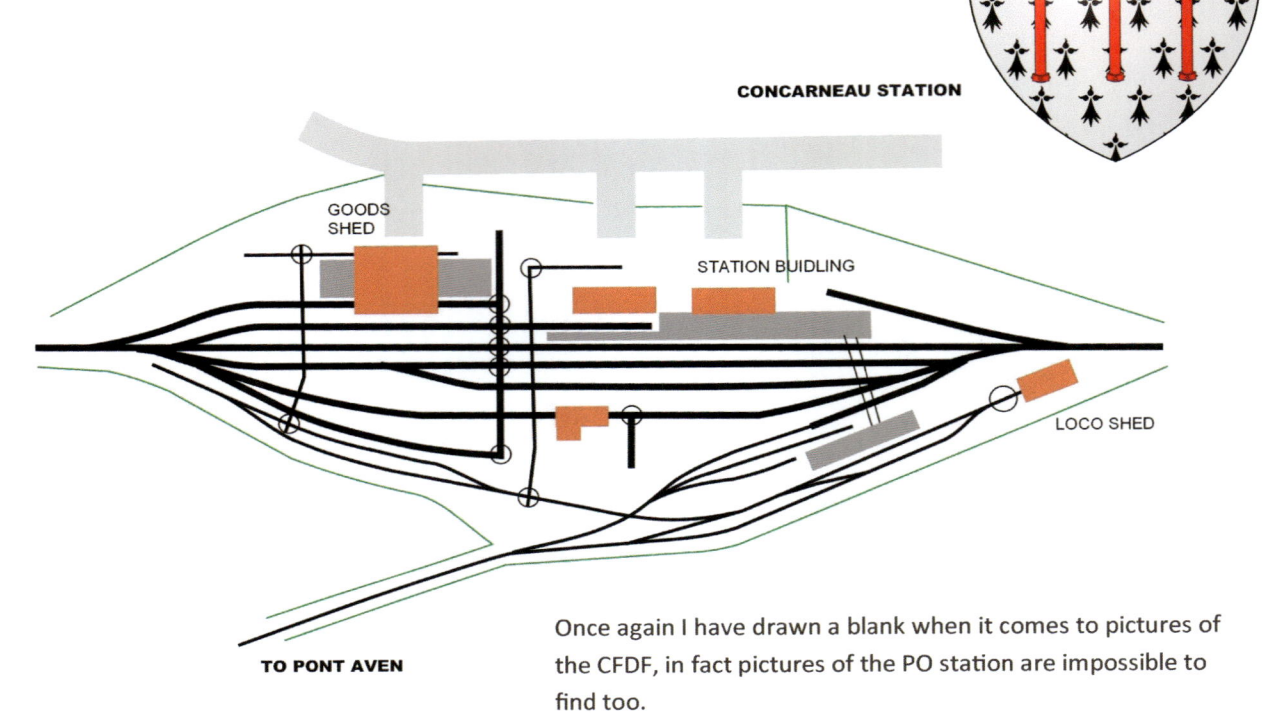

CONCARNEAU STATION

GOODS SHED
STATION BUIDLING
LOCO SHED
TO PONT AVEN

Once again I have drawn a blank when it comes to pictures of the CFDF, in fact pictures of the PO station are impossible to find too.

TREGUNC

Between Concarneau and Pont Avens was the village station of Tregunc.

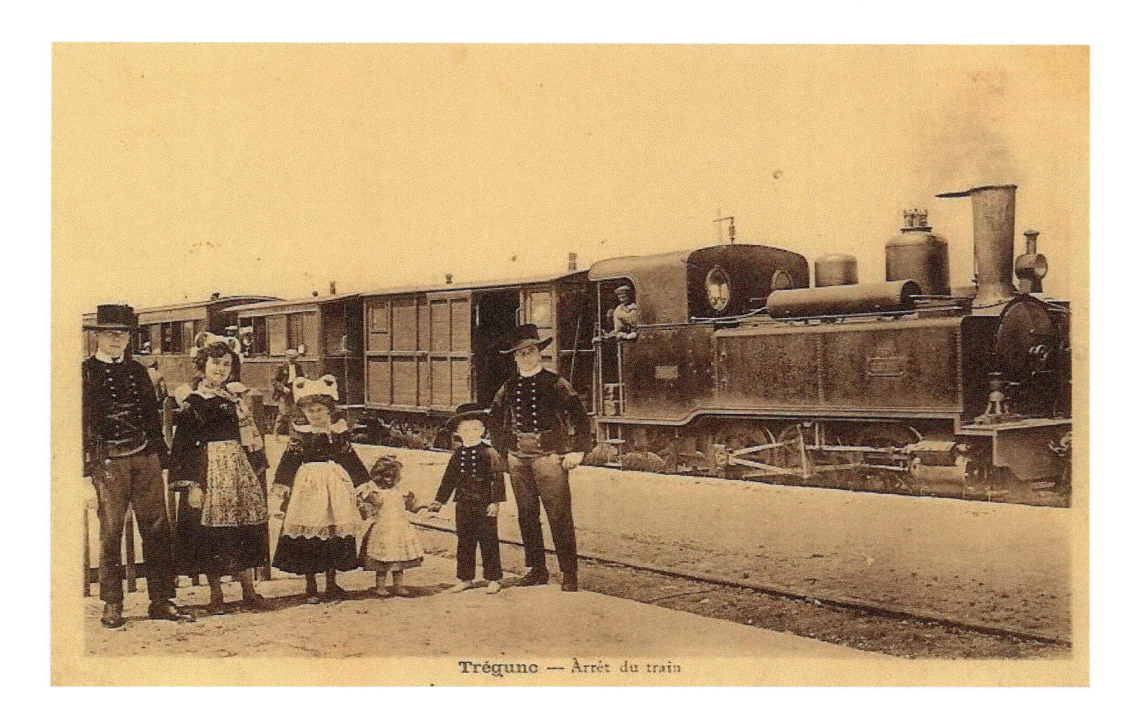

Trégunc — Arrêt du train

PONT AVEN

Pont Aven was a small town of three thousand six hundred people in 1906, and the main stopping place on the line. Thankfully it was better served by the postcard publishers, partly because of the attraction of this stone viaduct that took the railway across the river.

PONT-AVEN. — Le Viaduc

CHEMIN DE FER D'ORLÉANS

PONT-AVEN (FINISTÈRE)
La rivière à marée haute

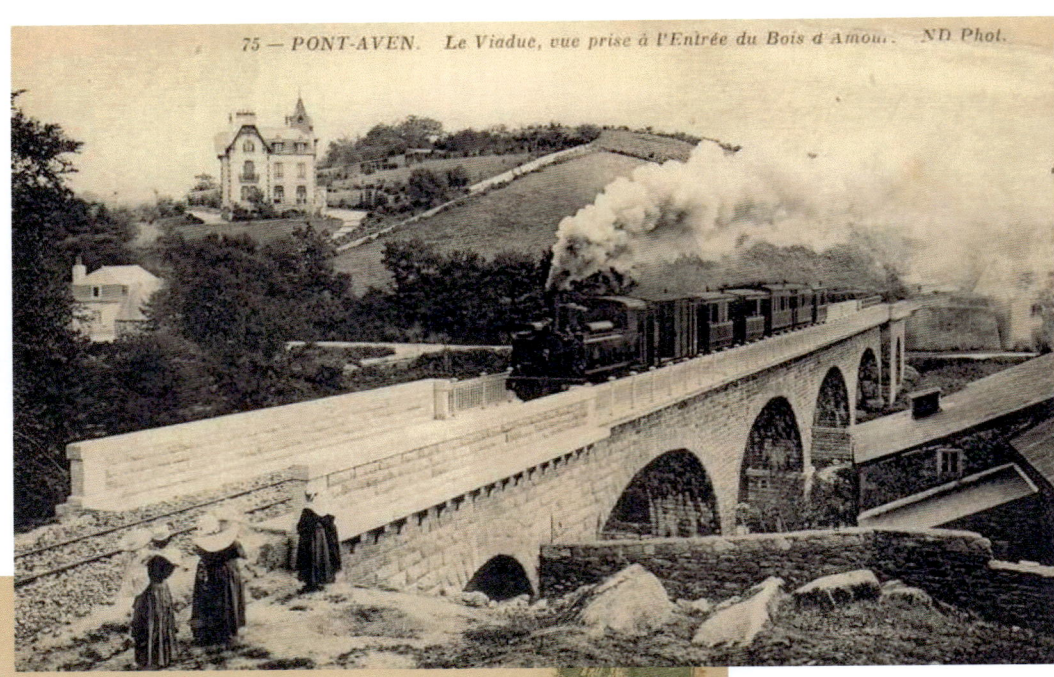

75 – PONT-AVEN. Le Viaduc, vue prise à l'Entrée du Bois d'Amour. ND Phot.

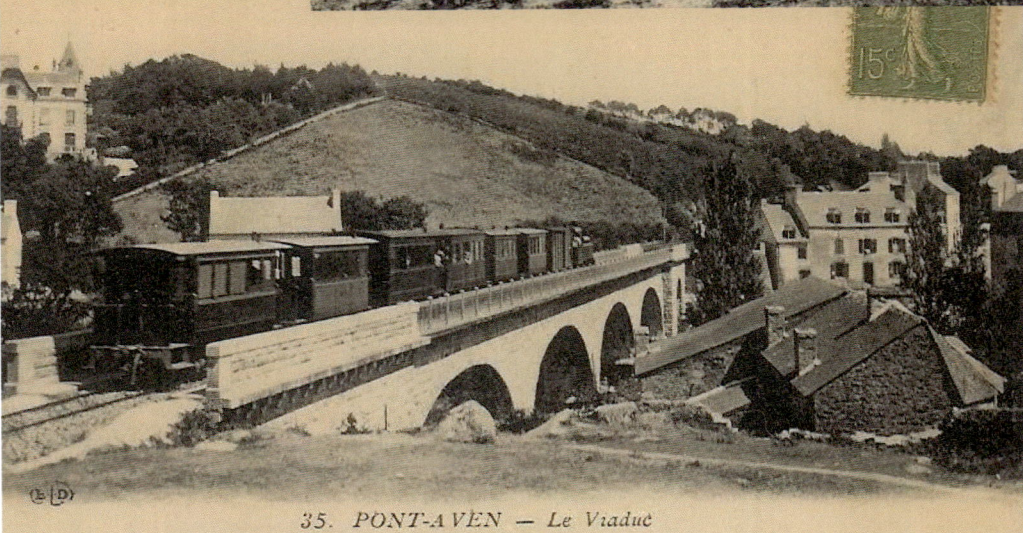

35. PONT-AVEN – Le Viaduc

– Passage du Train de Concarneau

PONT AVEN STATION

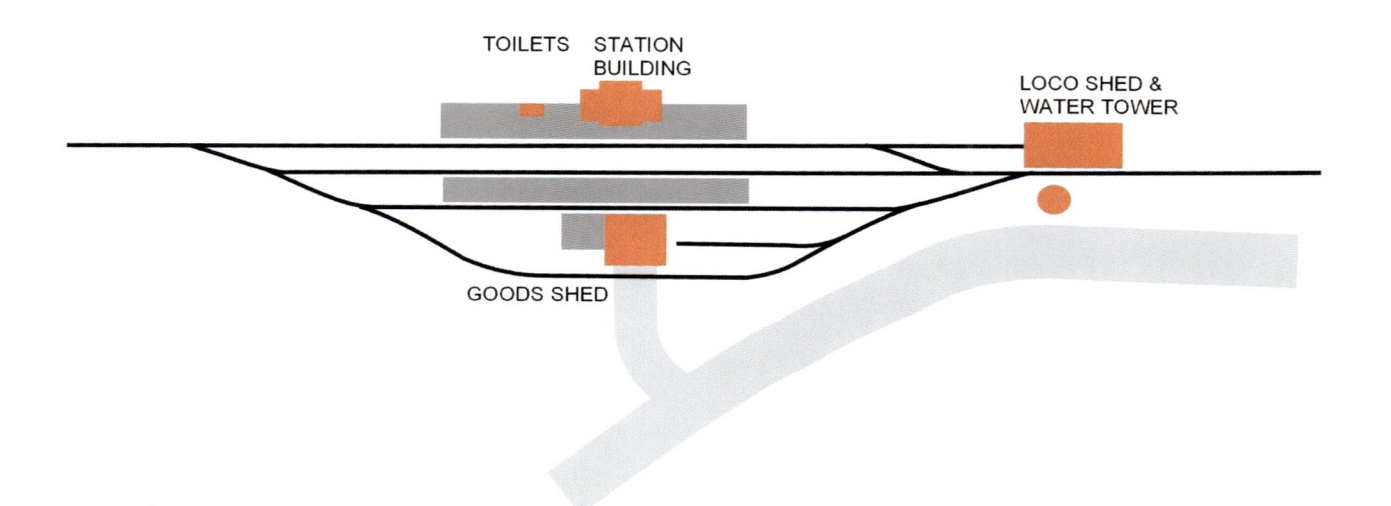

The simple station looks rather austere in this picture as the station building has been painted. Oddly the train is standing without a locomotive—maybe it was behind the photographer, perhaps taking water.

6055.- PONT-AVEN. - La Gare - Vue intérieure

If only we'd got a picture as clear as this for all the stations! The whole site is laid out before us, including the engine shed which would have been required for the five years that the station was a terminus.

62 PONT-AVEN. -- Vue sur la Gare. - LL.

QUIMPERLE

The line terminated at the P.O. station at Quimperle, which was on the main line from Lorient which opened on September 7th 1863. The town had over nine thousand people in 1906, and was an important destination for the railway to reach.

All the pictures I have are of the main line station, sadly. What a shame that the stripes of stone and red brick have been painted over on the station building.

I can't resist including this lovely picture! It is striking how nearly everyone was wearing what would now be considered the national costume, just to be worn on special occasions. In those days it was simply what you wore to go to work.

PONT CROIX TO PONT L'ABBE

The stations at each end of this line have already been described; the line was opened on 1st October 1912 as part of the second network and closed in 1933. Intermediate stations served the villages of Ploneour, Pouldreuzic and Plozevet.

Pouldreuzic station, the buildings of which still survive.

The track plan is simply a loop, minimal facilities but sufficient to serve these tiny communities.

Plozevet station, looking very open to the elements on this exposed coast.

CHATEAUNEUF DU FAOU TO ROSPORDEN.

This is a continuation of the line described in the last section, which carried in due south from Chateauneuf to the town of Rosporden. The 39km long line opened on December 21st 1912 and closed in 1933.

An intermediate station served the village of Coray which had around two thousand seven hundred inhabitants when the line was in operation.

ROSPORDEN

Rosporden is a town of seven thousand people which was served by the P.O. main line between Quimperle and Quimper. The main line opened in 1863 and the arrival of the CFA in 1912 is unlikely to have made much impact on the town although it did open up an area that had not had easy access to a station previously.

Rosporden was also reached by a line of the Reseau Breton from Carhaix which opened in 1896 and closed in 1967.

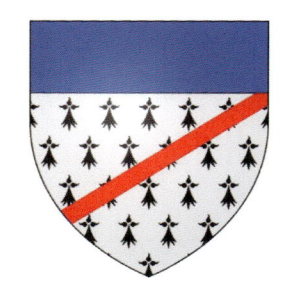

Rosporden P.O. station showing the distinctive architecture used on the line.

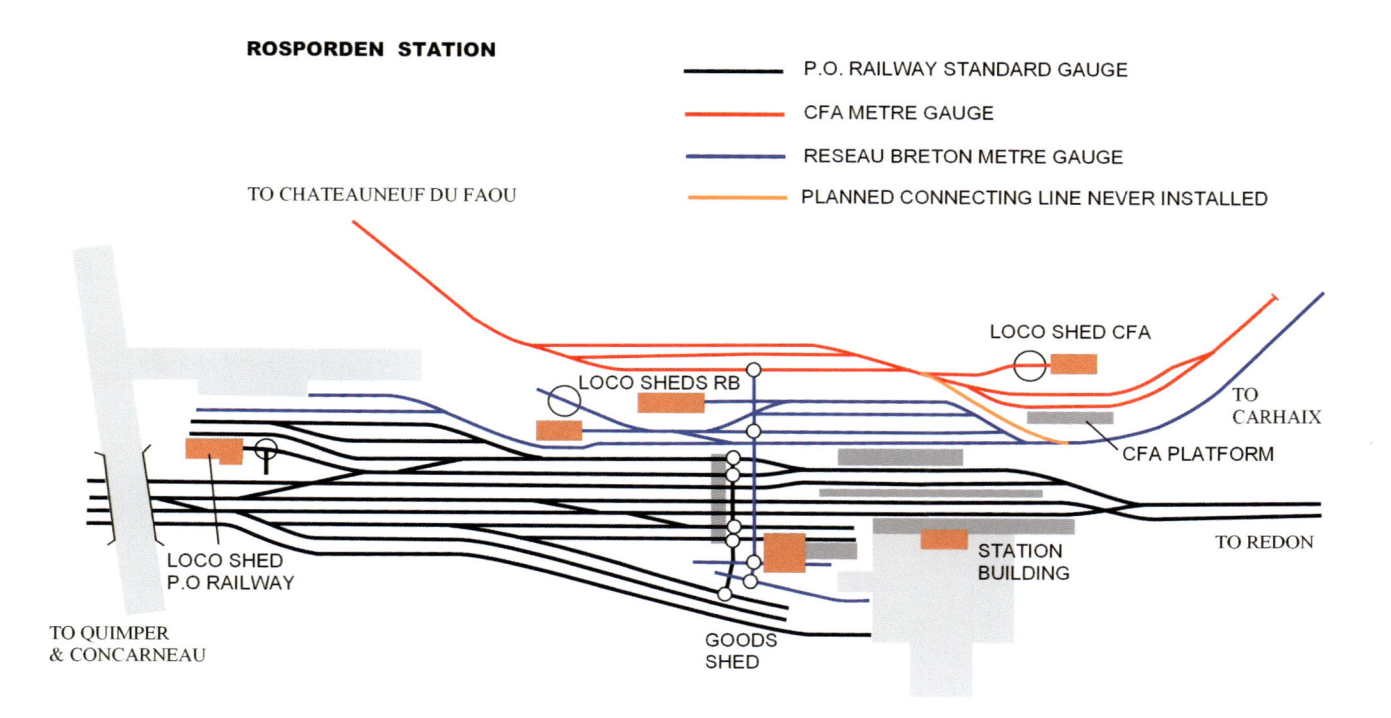

ROSPORDEN STATION

— P.O. RAILWAY STANDARD GAUGE
— CFA METRE GAUGE
— RESEAU BRETON METRE GAUGE
— PLANNED CONNECTING LINE NEVER INSTALLED

TO CHATEAUNEUF DU FAOU

LOCO SHED CFA
LOCO SHEDS RB
TO CARHAIX
CFA PLATFORM
TO REDON
LOCO SHED P.O RAILWAY
STATION BUILDING
TO QUIMPER & CONCARNEAU
GOODS SHED

1479. - ROSPORDEN. - La Gare

Collection H. L. M.

Trains in the Reseau Breton platforms.

Again, the CFA seems to have been ignored by photographers...in 1912 a new narrow gauge railway was no longer news as it had been ten or twenty years before. The CFA would have been on the grassy area to the left of the railcar.

104

BIBLIOGRAPHY

FINISTERE EN PETIT TRAINS   ALAIN DE DIELEVEULT   LA VIE DU RAIL

THE RESEAU BRETON   GORDON GRAVETT   OAKWOOD PRESS

LE RESEAU BRETON   CONNAISSANCE DU RAIL 2004

YOU MIGHT ALSO ENJOY THESE BOOKS BY PETER SMITH:

NARROW GAUGE ON THE COTE DU NORD

CHEMINS DE DER DE LA MANCHE

NARROW GAUGE IN THE DROME AND VAUCLUSE

THE RAILWAYS OF CHARLEVILLE MEZIERS AND THE FRENCH ARDENNES

THE THONES TRAMWAY

THE THIZY TRAMWAY

THE MAYENNE NARROW GAUGE

THE RAILWAYS OF HAUTE SAVOIE.

Printed in Poland
by Amazon Fulfillment
Poland Sp. z o.o., Wrocław